The Six-Pack Mind

Trevor

Trevor Keiran Crowley

© Copyright 2023 - All rights reserved.

The content contained within this book may not be reproduced, duplicated or transmitted without direct written permission from the author or the publisher.

Under no circumstances will any blame or legal responsibility be held against the publisher, or author, for any damages, reparation, or monetary loss due to the information contained within this book, either directly or indirectly.

Legal Notice:

This book is copyright protected. It is only for personal use. You cannot amend, distribute, sell, use, quote or paraphrase any part, or the content within this book, without the consent of the author or publisher.

Disclaimer Notice:

Please note the information contained within this document is for educational and entertainment purposes only. All effort has been executed to present accurate, up to date, reliable, complete information. No warranties of any kind are declared or implied. Readers acknowledge that the author is not engaged in the rendering of legal, financial, medical or professional advice. The content within this book has been derived from various sources. Please consult a licensed professional before attempting any techniques outlined in this book.

By reading this document, the reader agrees that under no circumstances is the author responsible for any losses, direct or indirect, that are incurred as a result of the use of the information contained within this document, including, but not limited to, errors, omissions, or inaccuracies.

Table of Contents

INTRODUCTION 1

CHAPTER 1: THE MAGIC OF HEALING 9

- LOVE YOURSELF BEFORE THEM ALL 15
- PUT THE BAGGAGE DOWN 19
- THE DARK WORLD OF TRAUMA 20
- THE POWER OF DESTRUCTION 22
- THE MAGIC OF HEALING 23
- YESTERDAY, TODAY, AND TOMORROW. 25

CHAPTER 2: TIME TO CHANGE YOUR THOUGHTS 29

- THE POWER OF THOUGHTS AND OVERTHINKING 30
- THE SPIRAL OF OVERTHINKING 32
- THINK, BUT DRAW THE LINE 34
- THE 4 PS THAT CAN CHANGE YOUR LIFE 37

CHAPTER 3: YOUR BODY'S A WONDERLAND! 43

- PHYSICAL BENEFITS 45
- MEDICAL BENEFITS 47
- EMOTIONAL BENEFITS 49
- PERSONAL AND SOCIAL BENEFITS 51
- BONUS BENEFITS 54
- TIPS TO ENSURE WORKOUTS IN A BUSY LIFE 55

CHAPTER 4: HOW "NOT" TO BREAK A LEG 59

- CARDIO 60
- STRENGTH AND WEIGHTS 63
- BALANCE EXERCISES AND YOGA 66

CHAPTER 5: NURTURING YOUR MIND PALACE 73

- THE IMPORTANCE OF MENTAL HEALTH 75
- WORK OUT YOUR MIND 77
- CLEAN, DUST, AND MAINTAIN YOUR MIND PALACE 93

CHAPTER 6: LESSONS FOR LIFE THAT NO ONE TOLD YOU ABOUT 95

- Time and Money on Your Balancing Scale 96
- Response and Reaction 98
- Be Who You Look Up To 102
- Working on Human Relations 108

CONCLUSION 113

REFERENCES 121

Introduction

The year was 1943. American psychologist Abraham Maslow wrote in his work *Theory of Motivation* about an average human's hierarchy of needs. This work changed the way the world looked at human needs and priorities. According to this work, the basic or the lowest tier includes the physical elements needed for our physical organs to function. They are food, water, and rest. Once the stomach is full and the body hydrated and rested, a human being then starts to think of how safe they are in their immediate surroundings. The second tier includes the need to feel secure and safe and the assurance to pull their guards down and relax. Once these basics are in place, a human being starts to seek a human touch in life in the form of intimacy, love, companionship, belongingness, and friendship. Now, they want to feel loved and yearned for. After this comes the fourth tier, which makes a person seek respect, importance, prestige, and acknowledgment. What this means is that the person now wants to be recognized as an individual and known for their own identity. The final tier, which most of us don't even reach, is about spiritual consciousness and awakening.

This is how humans realized the need to prioritize what is more important and what comes first, although this generic model varies slightly from person to person. Now, the year is 2023, about 80 years since Maslow defined how our standard steps of priorities work, but not much has changed in the application of the theory. As a child, I had the luxury of food on the plate or even intellectual fodder to feed my brain, but I missed having a place of security, comfort, and assurance from my father. He was himself drowned under an ocean of trauma from multiple repetitions of sexual abuse as a child. His past baggage pushed him to alcoholism and other self-destructive habits, which then fell on us kids like a blanket of darkness. So, while some parts of my needs were fulfilled, some remained either untouched or tarnished. I have seen and understood from life that a healthy body, sensible mind, a strong support system of people, contentment in work-life, and intellectual involvement are all important for one's holistic well-being, and each of these things can affect others. So, in this book, I have pulled up the highlights from my research as a writer and my experiences as an artist who grew flowers on infertile soil. No matter where you are at the moment, remember that life is beautiful, and I will tell you how.

Your mind is like a vast and expansive sky that walks with you wherever you go. But while you can hide in the comfort of your home when there is a thunderstorm in the sky, a storm in your mind will always take you over. You can run and hide from everything that is external or outside your body, but your mind is inside you. Nothing in this world can make you suffer more than your mind. There could be suffering everywhere—at deaths and departures, at funerals and weddings, at knee injuries and heartbreaks, and at daybreak and twilight. But if you train your mind right and can keep it covered, you are capable of letting nothing affect you. For instance, most of us have been heartbroken in love at least once in life. Think about it. It is never the person that you really crave but the way they make you feel. It could so happen that you might run across the same person years later and feel nothing. Why? It's because that feeling is gone, and your mind does not get the same signals you used to get from them. See the power of the mind?

We often find ourselves powerless in front of how our minds make us feel. We sulk about unresolved issues from the past that are not present anywhere but in our memories and worry about upcoming events that might or might not happen. In the process of worries, regrets, and pondering, we forget to live in the moment. Time is fleeting and never stands still for you. If we lose the moment, we never get it back. We anyway have limited time in this world as mortals. Can it be a good idea to lose out on the most precious gift called time? I always keep saying: Seize the moment.

Now you are wondering, who is this man to tell me how to use my time? True. Let's talk about that. I am no spiritual healer nor a life coach. But I am a man in the twilight of life who has been there and done that. I am merely here to share experiences from my own life and can only hope they help you.

My recent habit of hitting the gym, getting into spiritual practices, looking after my mind and body, and living life more consciously instead of cautiously has brought me a lot of joy and added a lot of value to my life. Buddhist monks say that we are not important as individuals. We are all merely guests here. So, mindfulness is great, but being overtly cautious can also damage things. You also need a few steps toward mindlessness, where you can create a vacuum in your mind, which you can fill with raindrops on roses and whiskers on kittens or whatever your favorite things are. Saving money in the bank is only essential for survival, but saving good thoughts and self-belief in your head is nonnegotiable. You will probably know all of this as you grow older, but if you read this book, you probably won't need to wait that long.

Patience and presence paired with kindness, compassion, and consciousness can bring great rewards in life. Start with looking at the mirror and telling yourself how lovable and precious you are. Most people forget to love themselves. Once you start showing compassion to yourself and the people around you, half your problems will be solved, and you will start to flow and flourish. Baggage from previous lifetimes and generations needs to be wiped, and underlying trauma needs to be healed. This way, you can break the pattern and start a new life. It needs courage and conviction, but the process will pay off.

Your breath can change your mind and the message that your body sends to your mind. Even during the most difficult times, you can convince your mind that you are relaxed by simply breathing in the right way and hence get rid of all anxiety and stress, thus inviting a better mood. What you can hold in your mind, you can hold in your hand. Changing habits formed through practice and genes can be hard, but patience and confidence can get the job done.

How often have you found yourself scrolling through the pages of a book and thinking about an upcoming presentation? Have you been in between a conversation and missed out on a few lines because your mind was busy with what you read in the news? Have you been on a vacation with family and constantly sulking about how you hate your office? It's okay! We are all guilty of being distracted at times. But if this happens too often, you probably need to know this. If you have faked your presence in situations, an average person will take less than a second to notice your delay in response or reaction, and an observant person even less. We think we can fake listening, but it originally damages relationships and moments. If it's not another person and just a book, movie, or vacation you are dealing with, do you think you can do justice to your experience if your mind is elsewhere? If you are not living your experience, what value does your experience add anyway? In this book, you will find some easy and accessible techniques to bring your mind in control and be present where you are.

I am not a storyteller nor a life expert. I have not done everything right. People have been mad at me and have left me many times. I have broken hearts and got mine broken. I have been unreasonable to people and been treated unreasonably. I have ignored people who loved me and valued opportunists for years. I have been wrong, and I have been wronged. But then you can ask, why Trevor, are you the right person to tell me how I should live my life? The answer is simple. Because I have been there and have gone through it all myself; I know what it feels like. I know how difficult it is to pull yourself out of bed for that morning workout. I know how hard it is to say no to your favorite doughnuts and choose fruit juice instead with no added sugar. I know how difficult it is to draw boundaries when you spot a toxic person and yet want to be around because they validate your existence temporarily. I know how skillfully you need to balance your weight when you decide how to spend your precious time, money, and efforts and distribute them among people and departments of your life. Did I ever say it was all going to be a cakewalk? No. They won't be easy, and there is no *shortcut in 13 days*, as many YouTube videos might tell you. All I am saying is, if you promise not to give up and hold my hand instead, we can make it together and reach the rainbows.

Let's go.

Chapter 1:

The Magic of Healing

Adam is a happy young boy. At 16, he excels at academics, sports, and other extracurriculars. His parents believe in his capabilities and have big dreams for his future. He wants to be a doctor and might be eligible for government scholarships by virtue of his academic credentials as well as excellence in sports. He is good-natured, and his neighbors and family friends adore him. A few members of his extended family talk behind his back, but that is a mark of a great performance by itself. The world sees Adam's parents gleaming with pride and Adam confident of bringing changes in the world he wants to see. But most nights when he goes to sleep, he feels bouts of anxiety. These sometimes lead to panic attacks that do not let him sleep all night long. He does not know what sparks his restlessness. He fails to realize what triggers such restlessness. At a tender and impressionable age, his perfect image is his only effective identity card. He doesn't want to upset his parents with a single mark on the beautiful moon that they happily exhibit. So Adam's mind decays, bit by bit, every night on his bed.

While the world rests in slumber,

Mother sleeps at peace,

Restlessly I toss and turn.

I can't see the bruises,

I can't see the cuts

But every night, I feel it burn.

Mrs. Dawson has been a wonderful homemaker, loved and cherished by her children. At the same time, she has been an impactful teacher who touched and changed many young lives. She wakes up by five in the morning and cooks and packs lunch for her husband, children, and herself. She takes the trash out and sometimes finds time to clean the house. Her children help her out as and when they can. They care for their mother deeply and get concerned about how she overworks at home and office. After handling a few chores at home, Mrs. Dawson leaves for school. She gives in a couple of hours for travel and eight more to teach at school. Apart from her subject, history, she also spends time with children after school for theatrics and musicals during competitions and concerts. She comes home late in the evening and quickly whips dinner for the family. Her elder son helps on most of the days. Finally, when she goes to her room with her husband at the end of the day, they perform the sexual rituals meaninglessly, as they have been doing year after year. She has dreamt of sleeping in her own room for all these years. She has wanted to listen to her favorite bands from her hometown and dance to herself to sleep. She would probably write a journal or use the privacy to call up her sister for a hearty chat. It's been years since she has cooked herself a meal that is *since* favorite and not her family's. It's been years since she has called herself Marie instead of Mrs. Dawson. She keeps staring at her husband and wishes he understood her a little after countless attempts to talk and solve their piled-up issues over the years. Mrs. Dawson's soul decays bit by bit.

Running around like a shrew

Fearing a stampede on the road

The cracks in my heart get bigger.

Do you see it, too?

I wither, crumble, and scatter

Marlow is a 30-year-old IT professional working at a swanky office in the Silicon City. She has never been a very bright student but has thoroughly enjoyed coding for her programmes. Her office provides lunch, nap time, and even flexible work hours inside the campus for the employees to socialize and chitchat. She leaves home early in the morning and enjoys spending all her day at the office. She is also paid enough to afford a nice apartment overlooking the better part of the city, where she does not get to spend much time. In addition, she started to get comfortable with not talking to her family for weeks as she kept drowning at work. Marlow was enjoying her life and chasing her big dreams. But recently, her colleagues noticed her stretching and shaking her arms too often, even during client meetings. After being confronted in a few days, she admitted that her arms and hands would feel heavy too often. Marlow delayed her doctor's appointment and the tests she asked her to take. When nothing seemed clear, but the symptoms persisted, she was asked to stay at the hospital for a few days for a thorough check-up. This, she delayed even further, partly in nonchalance and partly in the fear of missing out on the progress of her projects. After all, what would be more important than her job? Gradually, her feet also started to get heavier, along with her hands. She now felt lethargic to go for a walk. Soon, the bomb was dropped. Marlow's body decayed bit by bit.

In the rat race of life

I've got to survive!

Thunder, lightning, or rain,

It is time for deadlines again.

With arms so heavy and eyes so tired,

I will keep going. That's how I am wired.

Adam, Mrs. Dawson, and Marlow are all exhausted. They are tired of standing up to expectations—performance pressure from society, dreams in their own eyes, and assumptions of their dear ones. One battles anxiety—maybe a mental health issue—another fights marital issues, and the last one battles medical issues. Dear reader, can you identify one common element all these three people are dealing with? This element is the lack of diagnosis of the problem. The first step to healing anything is locating the exact problem.

Here is what happened next. Adam failed to appear for his final exams because of a severe anxiety attack that had remained untreated for years. Mrs. Dawson hung herself one night when she was finally alone because she could not take the weight of expectations and fakeness anymore. Marlow was diagnosed with Cervical Myelopathy, which meant a vein in her spinal cord was hardening and choking the other veins to death. She got the surgery done to fix it and could put a halt to probable paralysis, but she could never perform at work like before again, at the vibrant age of 32.

Now, here is what could have happened. If Adam had garnered the courage to talk about his insecurities, seen a therapist, engaged in relaxing hobbies, and delved deeper into his consciousness, he would have found out more about his childhood. He was forcefully taken away from his maternal grandmother after being raised by her for five foundational years of his life when his parents were away for work. Discovering later that his grandmother had died and that he would never see her again, he retracted into an imaginary shell and took refuge in academics. Gradually, he began to keep his mind busy with multiple activities throughout the day for the wrong reasons. In reality, what he was trying to do was escape the trauma of having lost what he craved. With the right treatment at the right time, Adam might have scored a little less than he did but would have lived a better life and breathed a little more.

Mrs. Dawson tried to speak to her husband many times in the past few years. He never bothered to really listen. He was borderline narcissistic and did not agree with the probability of him being wrong. Conversations stopped between them, and the sexual relations were more demanded and supplied rather than enjoyed. If she could have spoken up for herself louder or at least tried to take some time out to do things she really liked from her insanely demanding schedule, maybe she would have lived a little longer and better. The lady got tired of delivering like a superhero and gradually lost the energy to fight. If she could have gone to the depth of the issues in her marriage, maybe solutions would have sprung up.

Marlow was a young woman who got attacked by an unseen disease while she was too busy working. If she had been a little more conscious of the importance of medical tests and physical health, she would have been able to reverse the disease much sooner and avoided the surgery and the aftermath that came along. Her body could never forget the physical trauma that one single vein put it through. If she had taken out a little time every day for her health with practices like yoga, she might have been able to fight this better. If she had taken a little time to connect with family more often and shared about her physical issues, maybe they would have pushed her to get the tests done earlier. Life and health could have been different for Marlow.

Love Yourself Before Them All

So, what is this hullabaloo about self-love all around us? You might think: People have lived in communities and looked out for each other for ages. Why is it suddenly important to place your importance above everyone else's? Let's break this myth first. Self-love is not about selfish motives but about working for one's own happiness. Times have changed, and so has the world. Our work lives are complex, dynamic, and competitive today, and our families are nuclear. In today's world, the importance of focusing on one's own needs is of essential importance. Here are a few things self-love can help you with:

- By practicing self-love, your self-image can become more positive and your self-esteem more boosted. It impacts your mental health positively and can thus contribute to reduced levels of anxiety, stress, and depression.

- If you love and value yourself more, you will automatically be more resilient. You will be able to handle the challenges, setbacks, and disappointments thrown by life with more confidence and make lemonades out of them lemons easily without breaking down at little hurdles. You will be able to bounce back sooner and remember how life is beautiful regardless.

- Only a happy person can keep others happy. When you love yourself, you will be mentally equipped to have healthier relationships and maintain them effectively. Because you will be more aware of what is healthy and what is toxic, you will be able to build boundaries and communicate effectively to solve problems. Your choices will be more aligned with your happiness and health.

- Self-love can motivate you to do better and drive you to perfection without feeling the pressure to perform unreasonably. When you ascribe enough value to yourself, you will be willing to invest energy, time, and money in yourself and consciously engage in activities that help you to grow in your personal and professional areas. Productivity and success can grow in leaps and bounds hence.

- Apart from mental health, self-love directly helps promote physical health, control your basic medical statistics, keep your hormones balanced, and push you toward behaviors that are healthier for you. The motivation to eat the right food and exercise as per the requirements of your body can be boosted by self-love.

- A sense of self-love can keep you happy at all times and help you overlook little troubles that we all face every day. When you appreciate yourself and accept yourself as you are, others commenting adversely or things not working out have a lower chance of affecting you negatively. Furthermore, you would find joy and satisfaction in activities and people you engage with.

- When you love yourself and value your own emotions, chances are higher that you will also show more empathy and compassion for other people. When you are kind to yourself, you will also automatically feel more empathy for others and have the intent to foster positive connections.

- Personal development and scope of growth increase when you love yourself. They will keep you excited about good things and encourage you to look within yourself and explore your potential. They will enable you to pick up learnings from experiences and improve in the process rather than sitting back and sulking.

- When you engage in positive conversations, you will automatically have less intent and time to engage in negative talks, like sulking and whining about your life and talking negatively about other people. As they say, great minds discuss ideas; average minds discuss people.

- Finally, when you love yourself enough, you will live your authentic life. You will be able to stay true to your core values and beliefs and stick by your dreams and aspirations rather than spending too much effort on pleasing others.

From mental to physical health, hobbies to relationships, and dreams to goals, everything becomes a little easier when you love yourself. If self-love becomes an obsession, though, there is a need to draw a line. But we will come to that later.

Put the Baggage Down

Some of you might have heard this story, but let us run through it together. A professor had asked a classroom full of students the weight of a glass of water. One girl got up and talked about an interesting philosophy. She said that the weight of the glass of water can't be measured in metrics. The first minute of holding the glass can feel easy. In the next few minutes, the glass will start to feel heavier. After half an hour, the same glass with the same weight can feel much heavier and almost impossible to hold.

It is the same thing in life. If you carry old baggage with you for too long, it will seem heavier and heavier with time. This is why healing is so important, which we will discuss at length going ahead.

Whether you have been beaten mercilessly as a child, whether your heart has been broken time and again in school days, whether you have faced bullying and abuse or suffered from a lethal disease for years, there are ways to deal with all kinds of trauma. When you don't heal trauma early on, it starts taking the shape of heavy baggage and keeps bogging you down. Even simpler things in life like losing touch with your best friend, witnessing too much fighting in the house or violence in the neighborhood, or eating a vegetable every day that you despise can be causes for lifelong trauma and can keep interfering with your normal life every now and then.

Trauma management doesn't happen in a day and can take years to control and work around. But there is nothing that a strong and willful mind cannot do.

The Dark World of Trauma

The word *trauma* refers to "a situation where a person reacts to a certain stimulus adversely owing to a previous negative experience." When an event psychologically takes you over and overwhelms you, there are some instant shifts and changes in the body, mind, and reactions of the person. These experiences can cause a gradual decline and decay in the mental, physical, and social health of an individual. As we discussed earlier in the story of the professor and his class, statistics say that around 20% of people who obviously carry the baggage of their past for too long develop a condition called post-traumatic stress disorder (PTSD) (The Recovery Village, 2023). This is a common long-lasting effect of trauma on the human body. When a particular incident happens too many times and affects adversely, it is called complex trauma and has a higher chance of leaving long-lasting effects. When you witness a situation that invokes trauma but is not subjected to it directly, it is called secondary trauma.

The Inception of Trauma

Trauma can be carried forward from incidents that happened a month back to far as experiences from childhood. Common reasons for trauma can be physical, psychological, medical, and environmental.

A few examples of sources of trauma could be the death or loss of a loved one, physical, sexual, or mental abuse, severe medical injury or conditions, natural disasters, unsafe environment at home or locality, political turbulence in the country, falling down or getting hurt as a child, getting bullied, insulted, or ignored, witnessing violence among parents, friends, or even complete strangers, etc.

How Trauma Starts to Show

The first step for trauma management, as we discussed, is to identify trauma. You need to keep all your senses open for pronounced as well as subtle hints that your body, mind, and behavior give you.

Some examples of emotional symptoms of trauma are denial, sudden emotional outbursts, bouts of anger, uncontrolled misbehavior, extreme intolerance, long-term sadness that could lead to depression, anxious feelings, intrusive thoughts, flashbacks, nightmares, excessive caution or hypervigilance, startled, guilt, and shame among others which can even lead to near-death experiences.

Some physical symptoms of trauma are racing heartbeat, lethargy, fatigue, paleness, lack of concentration, heaviness in muscles, chronic pain, chest pain, insomnia, headache, dizziness, etc.

Effects of trauma like panic attacks might seem invisible to others but might impact the person as severely as a heart attack. Emotional symptoms are not only difficult for the patient dealing with trauma to handle but also for their loved ones, as it becomes increasingly difficult when they do not allow any help.

Trauma cannot be tracked or measured through medical tests or any tangible metrics, but the impact it has can completely jeopardize human lives.

The Power of Destruction

Trauma is extremely powerful. The effects it has on a human body, mind, and soul can be short-lived or even everlasting. Sometimes, when a child is treated with ignorance, the ingrained insecurity of being abandoned may remain with them till their old age. This can not only give rise to several physical ailments and emotional reactions but might also make them undesirable to their partner, friends, and family. A simple event can break hearts and families for a lifetime. Apart from PTSD, anxiety, depression, borderline personality disorder, and others are also possible effects of trauma.

Though trauma is powerful, the power of resilience and efforts in the right direction can overpower it altogether. When treated earlier, trauma can be managed better. If left untreated for too long, it can destroy health and life.

Even beyond a medical situation of trauma, people can just be careless about their physical health, hygiene, nutrition, physical activities, mental health, social circles, love life, family relationships, habits, concentration, behavior, and everything else that constitutes their lives. In this book, we will gradually learn how to combat the bad habits we have, work on them, replace them with better ones, and consciously lead a better life for us and the people around us. If you keep reading for a little bit more, new doors hiding massive opportunities for growth, development, and happiness will open wide, and you will thank me later.

The Magic of Healing

Most of us think it is only diseases and major setbacks in life that need mending and healing. This merely just shows a lack of consciousness, awareness, and mindfulness. A broken heart is as important to heal and put ointment on as is a broken arm. Just because you cannot see the hurt does not mean the damage is nonexistent.

Let's think of a situation. Nancy was travelling to her aunt's house in the countryside with her parents on a weekend. She was 13 years old at that time. Her father used to overwork all the time and hence got sleepy on the way. The constant bickering and quarrelling between the parents also kept both of them irritated. Somehow, in the middle of conjugal fights and eyes closing in while driving, he hit a roadside billboard and crashed his entire family into it along with the car. Nancy survived the crash in the backseat, but she lost both her parents.

Ten years later, Nancy's broken limbs were now healed, and she could walk almost as before, but her ballet dancing had stopped forever. Her uncle and aunt, who had taken her in after the unfortunate turn of incidents, were happy to see her heal and sent her to school in Massachusetts. While everyone thought Nancy was now doing fine because her prosthetic legs had fit in well, no one bothered about the hypothalamus inside her brain, which now scared her in between sleep and kept her guards high up at the slight shift of events. Nancy was suffering from PTSD and most of her friends started to ignore her, merely considering her ill-behaved and rude. If little changes were brought in her lifestyle ever since the major event happened and if her aunt and uncle were aware enough to take her to a therapist, she could have dropped a lot of her baggage down, if not all. If her father had tried to strike a balance between work, health, and family time, maybe his eyes would have not tricked him into sudden sleep, and they would still have been a family. And if her parents had gone to therapy, maybe they would have even been a happy family. Little changes in lifestyle and being aware of your situations can often make or break life and the whole story.

Yesterday, Today, and Tomorrow.

Forget the baggage of yesterday, stop thinking about the worries of tomorrow, and start to focus on life as it is today. This golden rule can take you through many difficult challenges in life to a better world. If you think you are broken, remember that so are many others. There is no glory in holding on to grief and sulking about it, but a lot of satisfaction in taking life head-on and embracing the changes.

In ancient Japan, there was a common practice of joining called Kintsugi. The Japanese would take broken pieces of pottery and join them back to their original form. The one twist of surprise was that they used molten gold as an adhesive to join these pieces. The philosophical knowhow to take home from here is that nothing in life is permanent. Just like good times, good health, good friends, and loyalty might not be permanent, similarly, diseases, heartbreaks, deception, sadness, and bad times are not permanent either. So, when an incident breaks you into a million pieces, you don't need to remain broken. In ancient Japan, you would have been valued even more for the experience you now come with. So, the next time you feel too broken to gather yourself, remember that you deserve to be treated better and fixed with gold.

The simplest of things like meditating for 10 minutes every day, keeping physically active, resolving issues with your partner before going to bed, communicating your needs and setting the boundary at the right place, putting good food in your body, being consistent with your practices, setting your goals and keeping focused, trying to wear the other person's shoes, mending relationships where you can, journaling your thoughts and expressing them correctly, pursuing your hobbies, and surrounding yourself with the right energy, among other things, can change a lot in your present life.

Healing essentially means striving toward holistic well-being. It is a long-term process and cannot be attained in a day. It is not a destination you can reach and stay at but a journey that goes on forever—only the experiences and the levels keep changing. In this book, let's talk about the little things about life and the big, the better days of life and the worse, and the best habits to take up and the worst.

In the next chapter, I will come back with a special gift of the 4 Ps. Are you wondering how weird it is? Keep thinking if these Ps are pineapples, peonies, or poems, and meet me on the other side. Together, let us discover the basic secret that no one tells us about the gap between anticipation and achievements.

Ready?

Chapter 2:

Time to Change Your Thoughts

Theists ask, why does God punish me all the time? Atheists, think why are people mean? Spiritual people wonder why the Universe is so harsh to them among everyone else. But let me tell you, if everything you are doing is working against you, it is you that is the problem.

Whether you talk about the *Universe*, God, or something else higher than you, anything beyond you responds to your vibrations. The higher power does not understand your mother tongue. They cannot understand the language you speak in. What they respond to is the vibe you emit. this is exactly how prayers, mantras, and manifestations work to make miracles happen for you. That is why the highest minds in the world have always said you are what you think.

Before we step into other habits in the next chapters, let us start with thoughts. The fastest traveler in the world and the strongest storyteller and cheerleader are all thoughts—more powerful than you know. It is a thought that let the Wright brothers discover that a human-made machine called the airplane can fly like a bird and a thought that allowed James Watt to imagine that steam could push a train forward. Thoughts are what form the base of any civilization moving ahead. But when the same thoughts flow in the wrong direction, they can halt or even alter your course of achieving something.

Thinking is one of the special cognitive skills humans have over other animals, and imagination is what sets us apart from them, giving us exposure to a broader life. But have you ever realized that it is these thoughts that make a person better or worse? A lot of times in life, whether because of baggage or intrinsic habits, people tend to think in the wrong direction and destroy the beauty of their lives and good experiences. Let us understand the pangs of overthinking in detail and how it can be overcome.

The Power of Thoughts and Overthinking

I have heard a very interesting story from traditional Sanskrit folklore, and I will start with that. A man once took a long walk and reached paradise by mistake. The walk was long, and he got tired. So, he wished he had a resting place around, and he suddenly saw a tree. This was the *Kalpataru*, or the wishing tree, which he had no idea about. He went and sat under its shadow and started to feel hungry. Then, he thought, I wish I had some food right now. Immediately, tasty and nutritious food across different cuisines was served to him from nowhere. He ate without extra questions. Then we wanted something to drink, and the best of drinks were served. In yogic traditions, an established mind that fails to make the right decisions is called a monkey's mind. The monkey in him kicked in as he could not understand where he was and how his thoughts were turning into reality in seconds—the same thing that people take years to attain with different kinds of manifestations. Then, he started to wonder that if all his wishes were coming true, there must be ghosts and demons around to make those things happen. And ghosts appeared from nowhere. Then, he thought these ghosts would surround him, torture him, and kill him. Then, that happened, too. What he failed to realize is that wishes come true in moments around the *Kalpataru*. In life, this tree is present anywhere beyond our knowledge. What you give to the Universe comes back to you. What this man did was ruminate and spiral in his own thoughts, thus inviting his own doomsday. Often, overthinking makes you attract problems that did not even exist originally.

The Spiral of Overthinking

Frequently, overthinking leads to problems that never even existed and to magnified versions of minor issues. It is a cognitive process that is common in individuals, where they dissect thoughts and delve into situations way deeper than they need. Overthinking can stem from different reasons.

Some people strive so much for perfection that they find themselves overthinking constantly about whether or not their performance is good enough, and they keep worried about making little mistakes. While perfection is an admirable trait to have, thinking about it excessively strips you of the natural flow of life and pushes you into the spiral of overthinking. My cousin is one such lady who likes her house prim and proper. In the constant obsession of keeping it tidy, her eyes hover around the table to find out flaws in how it is laid out at family dinners and also the exact taste of food. She automatically misses out on the fun of a family dinner. Also, no point in guessing that she's not the favorite aunt for the children who are scared of stares if the fork makes extra noise or the table cover gets soiled.

The fear of failing can make individuals overthink different probabilities in terms of consequences, which often leads to anxiety and fear. Some people may be so fearful of a negative result or a failure that they don't even try! For instance, I have seen people never telling their crush about their feelings lest they reject them. Can you imagine what a beautiful life could have been possible if they said yes instead or gave it a try?

Some people have a pattern of thinking negatively about everything around them. If a situation has five different optional outcomes, they will always think of the worst that can happen. I once read a story about a person who was so scared of the possibility of accidents that he never left home to avoid them. In a few years, a painting from the wall fell on his head, and he died in that accident. Would it not have been better if he had experienced life a little?

People who lack confidence in themselves often overanalyze situations, looking for validation, reassurance, and even approval from others about decisions in their own lives. This often happens due to the way they might have been brought up. These people constantly suffer from the anxiety of whether they are good enough or not. This lack of confidence made way for Jack at his office toward the promotion, which, ideally, Jerry deserved. But Jerry had done all the hard work night after night and failed to believe in himself and fight for what he deserved.

Some people just sit and replay scenes and situations from the past that might or might not have happened. These people ruminate and keep so attached to the past that they fail to connect to the present and plan for the future. This you will commonly see in people who have the luxury of free time, particularly at an older age.

Some people find it difficult to make decisions big and small. They are so unsure of their own selves that they take days to figure out what to wear for a party and probably decades to understand what product they want to produce to do business. Such people spend long hours thinking about the right thing to do every day and yet fail to come to a conclusion.

Think, but Draw the Line

So, if you have the habit of overthinking, in whatever magnitude, frequency, and tenure, do you just put life to a stop and accept things as they are? No. Here are a few ways you can bring a change to your life. Learn to focus on the current moment and live where you are instead of letting your mind wander across the world. This can be achieved with regular practice of meditation and mindfulness exercises. For instance, if you get into the habit of focusing on the nice time you are having with your spouse today instead of continuously pondering about how they did not help you with the errands last weekend, your relationship can move ahead, and better memories can be made.

If your mind automatically travels to the negative side of things when you think of consequences, start maintaining a journal where you write down in detail whether your conclusions are based on facts and verified data or random self-loathing assumptions. Then, ask yourself if you are assuming or concluding against an authentic source of information. This will help you understand that probably most of your pre-drawn negative conclusions and baseless. For instance, if you suffer from social anxiety and fear that the people at tonight's party will hate you, try and ask yourself questions like, "Is there a reason for them to dislike me so much?" Or, "Can I do something to have nice conversations with them today?" And, "What is the probability that I will not find a single person in a room full of people who would want to talk to me?"

If you think there is a pattern of mistakes you repeat and it has become a habit, start breaking them with small steps in the opposite direction. For instance, if you have been trying to quit drinking for years now and can't imagine your life without it, cut down from x number of drinking days to x-2, x-3, and so on. Once you are completely off this habit for years, you might be able to get to a place where you drink once in a while with friends and family to make merry. If the expectations are realistic rather than far-fetched, chances are higher for you to succeed.

Thoughts can be broken more easily by action than other thoughts. If you are stuck on the idea of doing something for a while, just get up and start doing it one fine day. If you write down the steps to be taken and start acting upon them, you have successfully broken the pattern of endless thoughts and are also closer to attaining what you want in life. If you think you might flunk the upcoming exam or not be able to crack an interview, utilize whatever time you have to study or prepare instead of thinking of what can happen.

Instead of overthinking about the problem that is bothering you, whether real or made up, start thinking about the probable solutions. When you think about solutions and, hence, better times, you will automatically feel better, release good hormones, and get closer to the best solution. Even if you don't find a solution to change the situation, thinking things are better can relieve you of stress.

If you are someone who always takes way too long to make a decision, give yourself a realistic timeline. Set a time limit and make a decision. Then, go by the decision and have faith in your choice. This will help you waste less time and learn to be confident.

If you feel nothing is working out in your stride, do not hesitate to look for support from friends, family members, and confidantes. The process will be gradual and might even be slow, but definitely rewarding.

Now, as promised, beyond all these simple tricks to follow to curb thinking in the wrong directions, I will present to you the 4 magic Ps that can change your life.

The 4 Ps That Can Change Your Life

The 4 Ps that we have such hype about are patience, presence, perseverance, and perspiration.

The first thing to learn for the growth curve of life is patience. When you sow a seed in the soil, you cannot expect it to turn into a plant overnight. When a woman gets pregnant, you cannot expect a child to be birthed immediately. When a lawyer starts practice, you cannot expect them to be an experienced advocate overnight. Most good things in life take time, and hence, patience is one of the biggest virtues for a human to learn.

Important milestones and goals often take time to attain. Patience is a must to keep committed and unmoved during the lengthy baking time of wait. If you cannot wait to see results, your efforts are often futile. To build and maintain healthy relationships, you need to give them time. This means spending time in making efforts and also giving it the time to process and ripen. Different people have their own timelines and own ways of things, and being patient about them helps you make your way through conflicts and strengthen your bonds. When you are patient, you will give time to any decision and the scope to collect information, see how things take shape, weigh out the different probabilities and options, and then make a well-thought-out decision instead of a rash one. Patience helps you handle challenges better when negative setbacks come your way. You need to look at negative situations with a calm and reserved mindset so that you can look for solutions rather than react. If you are patient, you will be able to pick up new skills, acquire knowledge continuously, and give that time and effort for your growth. Patience helps you battle the urge to give up during times of frustration. Patient people can manage stress, exhaustion, and anxiety with a balanced state of mind, and thus, they feel better in strenuous situations. Furthermore, patience can help you understand the views and perspectives of others, thus making space for smoother and more productive conversations. Patience suggests calmness and, subsequently, encourages your emotional well-being.

The next P is presence. A very important skill to learn is to be present in the moment you are living. If you are in a classroom learning a complicated theory of physics, no matter how exhausting it seems, it will help if you can train your brain to be present in the moment. When you are spending quality time with your family watching a movie on a Saturday night, you should try and keep all your worries about your workplace away and enjoy the moment only. When you are in the middle of a conversation with somebody, you need to develop the quality of being present and carefully observing as much as possible from that exchange. It is not only about the words they say but the way they say it, along with bodily gestures that support their expression. If you can be conscious of all the little details of that moment, you will understand from the moment what is being conveyed in words. When you offer your presence to a person, a project, or a situation in full, you make the most out of it and take home the best rewards. Even if the situation or the person is not the right one for you, your presence will help you identify that much sooner.

The third P is perseverance. It is deeply connected to patience. While patience will help you stay calm amidst a storm, perseverance would mean you have the zeal even at that moment to row your boat and sail on amidst the storm. Perseverance helps a person to be focused or even fixated at one point. Moreover, it helps one to hold on, achieve dreams and goals, invest time, have belief and confidence, overcome hurdles, build strength and resilience, adapt to new circumstances, be energetic about changes and challenges, inspire and motivate others, and walk toward long-term success. Perseverance helps a person build everything better—social circles, professional empires, a successful marriage, and many other walks of life.

Perspiration is the fourth and final P. This P means hustle. It stands for working hard for wherever you are headed in life but also working out and literally perspiring to balance your hormones, keep your body weight in check, and prepare better for a healthier old age. Figuratively, it stands for the hustle you need to undertake to reach anywhere in life.

Finally, all these 4 P's will lead you to a nice place, which is also another P. This P is the *promise* of a better life when you focus on the first four.

For all these Ps, one thing must work perfectly fine: your mind! So, before you blame any external power, whether your spouse, parents, friends, colleagues, or a higher power, ask yourself if you are doing enough to get what you want. Are you working in the right direction, and do you genuinely believe you are deserving of what you want?

Remember, the Universe has everything in abundance for everyone. You only pick up your share depending on what you believe is and should be yours. The law of attraction states that you will attract what you are and what you emit. Also, your actions have to be aligned with your thoughts. Thinking you deserve the person you love or the job you want and not acting toward it will mean a clash of energies, which will eventually lead to nothing happening out of the reaction.

Now that we know about the power of the mind, in the next chapter, we will talk about the last P or perspiration or the importance of working out your body. What do you think? Is working out and keeping fit a fad developed by social media influencers? Is it a way of life for celebrities who get paid to look good? Or is it essential for both the people writing the book and reading the book? What do you think? Read on to learn the secrets about how exercising can change your life!

Chapter 3:

Your Body's a Wonderland!

You might have heard this song a zillion times. When John Mayer sings it, you probably hear and stare equally in awe. But when a friend, a relative, or a random *wellwisher* comments on how your body is a wonderland that can perform wondrous activities when you treat it right, how do you react? Not very well, I am guessing? So, let's excavate some facts about the role of activities in your body.

Exercise, run a few miles, and keep fit are a few suggestions most of us get from different sources. Now, let me ask you today: Why do you think these are so important? Is it to build robust muscles and lift a 40 kg suitcase with one hand with ease? Is it to flash washboard abs when you flaunt a bikini during your summer trip to the Bahamas? Or is it to do 100 pushups and hold your body upside down in a headstand for a few minutes to win a talent hunt?

Let's talk about Kelly. Although they say a woman's age is not a topic of discussion, her age, which was 38, is relevant here. Kelly worked with me in my last office.

She was a perfectly healthy, slim, and fashionable girl with a pleasing personality working in the legal department. One fine morning, she spread her arms wide above her shoulders as she yawned and stretched during a long day at work. Everyone at the station heard a cracking sound followed by her shriek. She was in pain, and everyone knew it, but why? No one understood. As it turned out, she stretched her arms back, and her shoulder bone got dislocated. We rushed her to the hospital, and the treatment started immediately. Can you imagine the kind of lifestyle youngsters today are leading where they can literally be arm-twisted into dislocation with just a stretch?

If you do not realize it today, you probably will in a decade or more, depending on your age and health conditions, that lifting your own trolley bag, pushing a heavy door, or shoving snow from the backyard are all basic chores that need basic fitness and strength.

The world of flaunting and social media might have shown us very glamorous sides of workouts, but the reality is quite different. No one is denying the aesthetic bit, but we will come to that later on. Let us first discuss the basic benefits we get from exercising daily. We will divide these benefits into four different sections, namely physical, medical, emotional, personal, and social. Let's see you pick up the points from each section that seem important for you. Once we are done discussing all these points, we can take a call about how important exercising is for *you*.

Physical Benefits

- Regularly exercising helps control and maintain a healthy weight by burning extra calories. To hit a break-even point for a healthy weight, the amount of calories you intake every day needs to be less than the amount of calories you burn. A balanced weight not only helps you look better and fetch compliments but also promotes good health all over.

- With proper strength training exercises, you can see noticeable development in muscles and enhanced strength and endurance. When muscles get strong by themselves, your bones will not need to exert as much when they grow old and start to decay. If muscles are strong enough, they can support your bones. Your bones, which will obviously lose some strength as you age, will have a slimmer chance of giving you trouble if they have support from muscles.

- Cardio exercises like swimming, running, and other freehand exercises can improve the health of your heart and extend your life span by years. They increase blood circulation to all parts of your body and thus reduce the risk of cardiovascular diseases. A healthier heart is a marker of a longer lifespan, an improved immune system, and transportation of oxygen to the necessary areas of the body.

- Exercises for flexibility help in situations like Kelly's historical stretch and many others where a twist or push might give you an injury of a lifetime, sometimes damaging bones or tissues forever. When the range of motion is increased, stiffness is released from your joints. With smoother movements, you will be more confident in little things like putting a box of cereals on a higher shelf or extending an arm to hit the cock while playing badminton without fearing an injury. As they say, what doesn't bend, breaks.

- When you exercise your bones, with cardio and weights, the risk of osteoporosis and other bone diseases runs lower in older age. Especially in women, lack of calcium is very common from middle age, which gradually leads to joint pains followed by crippling immobilities.

- Because of the structure of life today, most of the younger generation is working on the laptop or staring at their phone screens for longer hours. Humans are slowly bending forward and starting to look like apes, their forefathers. This is a major problem in evolution today. When the core muscles tighten and the back is regularly arched backward to combat the regular bending down, the risk of musculoskeletal diseases lowers. Back pain and bad posture are also two common issues that can be resolved with exercise.

- Imagine getting off your bed at an older age and having to hold a stick to walk toward your toilet. Would you want to resort to that or walk down to the car and drive to the mall yourself for as long as you can? Exercise helps to maintain balance, focus, and coordination of the nerves and organs. It also helps you stand strong and avoid falling down, which is common in old people. Even if you accidentally fall sometimes, exercise will help you recover much faster. If Kelly had fallen down with that kind of bone strength, she would sure have broken a leg.

- Besides all other physical benefits, your energy levels can go up by leaps and bounds when you exercise in a healthy manner regularly.

Medical Benefits

- Regular exercise can reduce the levels of bad cholesterol in your body, which tend to go up given the sedentary lifestyle we lead these days. It also pumps blood better into the heart and keeps it thriving for longer, reducing the risk of different diseases and even untimely and sudden heart attacks we predominantly witness nowadays. Moreover, Blood pressure is controlled better with exercise, keeping the body immune to diseases in general.

- Type 2 diabetes, which sets the base for many lethal diseases, can be managed or even prevented with the right exercises.

- A consistent and regular habit of exercising can combat insomnia and promote the frequency and quality of sleep.

- The general immune system can be boosted with exercise, thus reducing the risk of various illnesses trying to make a home in our body.

- Certain kinds of cancer may be fought with exercise.

- Bone diseases like arthritis and osteoporosis and lung diseases like chronic obstructive pulmonary disease (COPD) can be kept away with an enhanced immune system.

- Cognitive functions generally take a dip and decline as the body ages. This means they may no longer retain information for long; they may process things slower and generally become less responsive, and they may not remain good at planning, organizing, and problem-solving. Even abilities like concentration and focus, which we take for granted, may be lost with time. All of this can be combated to a great extent with regular exercise.

- Exercise can keep your organs functioning better for longer and thus give you a longer lifespan.

Emotional Benefits

- By exercising, the body releases a few hormones that are collectively called the happy hormones. They are neurotransmitters called endorphins, dopamine, and oxytocin. These chemicals interact with receptors in your brain and take the message to your brain that you are relaxed and happy, reducing the feelings of pain and anxiety and promoting positive feelings.

- With exercise, the levels of stress hormones like adrenaline and cortisol are balanced and in control, reducing the feeling of stress and managing it better when it hits you.

- Even though you end up spending a lot of your energy on exercising, it adds to your energy levels instead of taking away from them.

- Your self-esteem and confidence are higher with exercising, and you mentally feel ready to take up challenges and face the world every day. Exercise also leaves you feeling accomplished and positive and paints a higher picture of yourself in your head.

- Not only during old age but during whatever age you are at, exercising can improve your cognitive functions like memory, concentration, focus, learning abilities, and understanding.

- If you suffer from mental health issues, regardless of the seriousness, like depression, anxiety, PTSD, ADHD, and others, exercising can distract your mind toward better things and keep you worry-free for long hours. If you focus on your breathing, movements, and sensations in your body during your workouts, you can give your mind a break from everything that causes tension.

- Taking up new challenges regularly during exercises and pushing your boundaries further can etch in your subconscious how powerful you are and thus make you resilient and tough. This helps you battle hardships with a lionheart, knowing inside that you will handle it.

- Finally, exercise can help the brain grow new neurons in it and connect them better with each other. The risk of mental health issues is thus lower, and the health of the brain is better.

Personal and Social Benefits

- Once you start exercising, there are lots of ways to interact with others via exercises. When you take part in group exercises, like fitness classes, sports, or hiking, soccer, skiing, rock climbing, and so on, you automatically get an opportunity to interact and communicate with strangers. You learn to be a team player and sharpen your social skills.

- Even if you are usually socially awkward and don't know how to strike up a conversation, these people are already interested in at least one thing as you, making the conversation starter really easy. Since you have a common interest, you can start talking on those lines and gradually find out what else they have in store.

- Team activities will help you develop skills like communication, teamwork, collaboration, interaction, cooperation, and others. These circumstances also help you learn how to support the other team members, celebrate victory, and accept defeat.

- Taking part in community events in the locality like marathons, charity runs, sports leagues, and so on, brings individuals together in a community and also sets up a social plane for them to mingle outside these events. They work as icebreakers for strangers. So, if you meet someone at yoga class twice and then see them at the local grocery, you'll feel more comfortable to go up and say hi.

- Try to take up outdoor activities like walking, jogging, cycling, hiking, or group walks if the walls of your office and home are feeling monotonous day after day. Even if you are not interacting, just watching a few other people actively enjoying their workouts can make you feel fulfilled. This helps greatly in cutting loneliness and monotony, which are both common new-age problems.

- Beyond physical competitions, you can also connect with friends and family across the globe through fitness apps that track all your movements, activities, and calories burnt to see who exercised and how much. This can promote healthy competition, which can act as a motivation for all of you to work out and also have constructive chats about them.

- People with anxiety, abandonment issues, and other insecurities can find a natural and spontaneous way to mingle with people and hence handle social anxiety without getting into the battle that they usually have to fight. This allows a free flow of interactions which feels less intimidating.

- A lot of people prefer to use these events and activity times as networking opportunities for business and professional connections. Playing squash, tennis, golf and other games, is a common meeting room for professionals to run, hit, and make money and connections.

- You can use your workout time to spend quality time with your spouse or partner if you are otherwise pressed for time. Going out to play a game or for a jog at the same time every day or every week sets a good habit for both of you and brings you closer, not just as partners in life or at home but also as a team. Healthy competition can create a little friction, which can spark sexual tension and solidarity, and a team game can make you feel closer as a strong team.

- You can use your workout time to bond better with your parents. If they live close by, take them out to physical activities curated for elderly people and give them the gift of strength and your time.

- Commit to someone like a coworker, friend, or neighbor—anyone outside the house to exercise with. Signing up with a personal trainer or a real-time group trainer is also an option, physically or virtually. The idea is to have someone waiting to start the session or give you a nudge if you miss your sessions often. This will keep you motivated and give you the extra push.

- Meet your friends at the weekends after work to play a game you guys might all like. You could also introduce each other to your respective forms of workouts.

  If you like Zumba, talk to your instructor and invite them for a session sometime. If someone goes for taekwondo, spend a weekend learning some basic moves if you like.

Bonus Benefits

Who are we kidding? No matter how shallow this sounds, we all would rather look good than not. And what is the harm? I am all in for body positivity in all shapes as long as the fitness quotient is in place.

So, no points for guessing this benefit. When you work out regularly, it starts to show. Your good hormones are pumped, and the glow is visible on your skin, the shine in your hair, and the smile on your face. Additionally, you will soon start to see a difference in your weight and shape. If you are within the right bracket of weight already, you still need to exercise for all the other benefits we spoke about. If your weight is higher or lower, you need to make efforts to strike a balance. Food is a major factor that we will talk about later in the upcoming chapters. So, all in all, exercise can fetch you a sudden rush of compliments and maybe a few cuties who come flirting more often than before.

I have been hitting the gym for some time now. The world suddenly seems better in look and feel, and so do I! What I have learned is that do not exercise to lose weight or look good. Do it for the fitness and the strength you can rave about. Aesthetics will follow!

Tips to Ensure Workouts in a Busy Life

I understand that not everyone has the luxury of heading to the gym at a decent time or going for a walk in the evening. Your life, work, and time schedule might not allow it. If you are struggling to find time and space to fit exercise into your schedule, here are a few tips to make life easier and yet keep you fitter.

- Schedule your workouts externally by adding them to your calendar, physically or virtually. If evenings are for work or travel and nights too hectic, try waking up an hour earlier than you do and give yourself at least half an hour of exercise. You will be surprised to see how energetic the day will feel. If you can consciously add this to your morning schedule, you will get hooked to your morning workouts soon and something will feel amiss when you don't get it.

- Choose the kind of exercise that you enjoy and stick to that for your daily dose. If you enjoy HIIT, you might not like to dance in a Zumba class. Try a few things and figure out what works best. Your choice needs to be sustainable so that you don't give up soon. For instance, if you are a social person, you probably won't enjoy solitary sports.

- If your timings at work are haywire, subscribe to a gym that runs 24 hours or sign up for online classes with multiple slots throughout the day. If your daily life involves a lot of travelling, try to hit the gym at the hotel you stay at or exercise by yourself in the room, asking for a yoga mat. Be ready with your gym clothes packed in your bag always to delve into any opportunity you might get.

- If your day is already packed, try to work out at home rather than travelling and wasting time heading to the gym.

- Walk the dog, go shopping for daily household items, and dress the garden. These are activities that will keep you fit and also get chores done.

- If you are shopping for cartons of juice or packets of rice, take a couple of them in both hands and lift them 10 times each in an upward motion before you keep them away.

- Try parking the car far away from your entry point at the parking area and walk to the door. The walk to and from the car can add well to your physical activity.

- Whenever you can, leave the car behind and walk or ride your bike to the destination.

- If the day at work has been too long and you're too late home to schedule a workout, get off the bus a couple of stops before your destination and walk the rest of the way.

- At the office, walk to your colleague's station to have a chat rather than email them.

- Make small hand and foot rotations when sitting at your workstation at a stretch, and make sure to get up from the chair to take a stroll every hour.

- Take the stairs to go up to any building instead of taking the elevator when possible.

Now that we know the benefits and tips of exercising, in the next chapter, let's learn the real drill. I will give you ideas for some varied exercises if you are new to this world. I hope you're charged up because I totally am!

Chapter 4:

How "Not" to Break a Leg

Our hunter-gatherer ancestors used to walk for miles every day to look for food and migrate from one place to another. They had to run around to save themselves from wild beasts, kill animals, light fires, and dance around them for community gatherings in the evenings. Even if we walk forward chronologically, our ancestors have had to push and pull levers, work manually as artisans and then at factories, chop vegetables to feed large communities or families, climb trees, stretch their hands and limbs two big fruits, work on all fours stealthily out of a dangerous situation, and so on. Even a century ago, they had to walk up to their rooms in houses and then apartments when there were no elevators. Day by day, I would say lifestyles are changing two words: what we call development and advanced versions of civilization. However, this is making us sedentary, providing us all the means to be lazier by the day.

As we discussed in the last chapter, exercising can change your life. But there are some more important things to discuss. You might have heard some people say that they don't need to lift weights because they are already going for a run every day. You might even get to hear that because somebody is a weightlifter, they do not need to worry about walking with a stick in their old age. I am sorry to burst that myth. I do respect that some people might enjoy swimming more than dancing, and some others might enjoy lifting in the gym more than cycling outdoors. It is okay to have preferences, but it is also essential to know that all these exercises come with different sets of benefits, and one is not to be confused with the others. Ideally, a mix of basic cardio, lifting, flexibility exercises, and exercises for strength and balance is great for the human body. While it might not always be possible to incorporate all of them into your schedule, let us get to know them in depth and make a conscious choice for ourselves.

Cardio

This is one of the most basic forms of exercise that humans have been doing since time immemorial. Doing any form of cardio exercise can improve your cardiovascular health by reducing the risk of heart disease and promoting blood circulation in your body. Cardio will have a basic contribution to weight loss, which is one of the biggest concerns in today's world, especially for privileged first-world countries. It helps to keep stress and anxiety levels in control and can boost your mood with the release of happy hormones like endorphins and dopamine. This happens as a natural result of an increase in breathing rate and heartbeat. Cardio gets the body tired and improves the quality and duration of your sleep. It helps you to fall asleep faster, still asleep longer, and maintain the regularity of your sleep cycle. Regular cardio exercises can increase your stamina and endurance and also prepare you for situations where you need to work out for longer periods of time at the gym or elsewhere. Chronic diseases like heart disease, diabetes and even some forms of cancer can be prevented with cardiovascular exercises, thus reducing the chance of premature death. Better flow of blood and oxygen to the brain can help you improve your concentration levels and see things with more clarity, developing your cognitive skills. By constantly working your lungs heavily and for long periods, cardio exercises help your body adapt to the rising demand for oxygen. Hence, your lungs become stronger and more efficient in times of need. Besides, by increasing your metabolism at the rate at which your body decides to burn calories, you are able to manage weight better.

Apart from basics like walking, running, jogging, swimming, skipping, dancing, and other sports we generally know of, here are a few simple and easy cardio exercises you can usually practice at home. You can start doing them in fewer numbers and fewer sets, which you can increase with time and increased endurance.

- Arm circles: Raise both arms on two sides and start making small movements. A few moments to try are making continuous circles toward the front, making continuous circles toward the back, and lifting and dropping your arms upward continuously with your palms facing the ceiling. As you do this, you need to stand straight with your tummy tucked in, shoulders pressed back, and the rest of the body still.

- Jumping Jacks: Stand straight on a yoga mat or on the floor, your feet together. Place your palms on the sides of your thighs. You are basically in the attention position. Now, with the count of one, race both your hands from the sides and take them up to clap ones and simultaneously push both your feet to their respective sides with the 2-foot gap in between. And the next count, bring both the feet and the hands back to their original position. Keep repeating this change of movements 10 times, to begin with, and increase the count with time.

- Air Squats: Stand straight with your hands folded together in front and your tummy tucked in. Keep one shoulder gap between both feet. You now need to move toward a sitting position but stop when you make a chair position. Push your hips downward but also backward so that you can see your toe when you look down. You're back should be straight at all times and pushed as backward as possible. If you are doing it right, the level of your hips will be lower than the level of your knees.

Strength and Weights

As we discussed before, just because you can run very fast does not mean you will be able to lift a heavy suitcase without spraining your back or pulling a muscle in your calf. Strengthening exercises have their own perks, which help you not only have stronger bones but also maintain worry-free youth and old age. With strength training, you can manage your weight, make your bones stronger, engage in different everyday activities and adventure activities without worrying about joint pain and injuries, grow old with less stress of having to depend on others, control the chances of chronic conditions like arthritis and osteoporosis, and even strengthen your brain cells to think better and sharper.

Apart from softly lifting household articles like a carton of milk or a bottle of water any time of the day, here are a few easy and simple strengthening exercises you can do with dumbbells. If you don't have them yet, there are numerous exercises available online that you can do with regular household articles like bottles, ropes, towels, your children, or even your own body weight. Always remember to start your session with some light cardio and stretching before lifting weights so that you don't pull a muscle, especially if you are working out in the morning. Here are a few strength training exercises for you:

- Weighted squats: Repeat the air squat from the section above and add a kettlebell in your hands as you hold it in front of the chest. No movement is required separately for the hands. If you want to add variety, try adding a different motion. After every squat, stand straight up, raise the weight high over your head, and bring it back down to your chest. Repeat a few rounds and keep increasing the number of sets and the weight with time and practice. Another simple version of weighted squats is to hold a dumbbell in each hand and simply perform your squat. The head of the dumbbells can be tilted forward so that it touches the ground every time you dip.

- Romanian Deadlift: Stand straight with your feet at a one-hip distance, a dumbbell in each hand, and your palms facing your body. Start pushing your buttocks back and slightly downward with your spinal cord straight at all times and your shoulders pushed back. Keep your core muscles and glute muscles very tight to get the best effects of the exercise. Keep your knees softly bent to reduce stress from your lower back and avoid injuries. As you push your hips back, lower the dumbbells with your arms straight and facing your body. The dumbbells need to be brushing down the length of your things and then your shin bone till the point where your hamstrings are slightly pulled. Increase in numbers and weights with time.

- Weighted push-ups: Push-ups are, by themselves, effective for strength training with your own body weight, but you can do them with disc weights on your back for additional impact. I highly recommend using your children to do this exercise for your own good and their fun. At an advanced level, people also try them with their partners. You need to lie straight on a yoga mat facing downward with two palms placed on two sides roughly beside your shoulders. Now, strengthen your core and raise the front of your body to a high plant position with your back parallel to the ground. Hold for a second and gradually go down. You can start with dolphin push-ups in the beginning or diagonal push-ups using a table or a bed.

Balance Exercises and Yoga

The benefits of balance exercises must not be forgotten in a world where everybody is running behind HIIT and cardio exercises for power and strength. Balance exercises and yoga set the base for your body's core strength. The ability of a body to balance itself declines with time and age. In fact, the tenure that a person can balance on one leg and be counted is a critical marker for stability. Your brain, muscles, and several parts inside the ear are involved in the complex skill of balancing. With time, the coordination depletes between these systems and makes it difficult to even walk steadily. Think of an infant trying to get up and stand on their own legs. An old person can falter in the same way. Standing upright is a skill we take for granted, but lack of balance exercises throughout our life again show us our place in no time, endowing the worst feeling of dependence.

Balance exercises help reverse your age and can track your body into thinking you are much younger than you are. Since you're poor and your limbs are more in control, even if you lose your eyesight and stumble upon something, you can quickly balance yourself and avoid a fall or an injury. Staying fit and rooted will also infuse a certain sense of confidence in you, which will show in your posture. You can keep reduced mobility, hunched shoulders, pelvic tilt, and other defects and posture away with regular balance exercises. A good posture is not even common among youngsters today because of the lifestyle we spoke about. Imagine how glamorous and convenient it will be to maintain a good posture at an older age!

With regular balance exercises, even if you happen to fall sometime by accident, you will recover from the injury much faster. With good balance, and especially with the practice of dynamic balance exercises like walking on a line of bricks with full concentration, you can develop better reflection of response and coordination. When your muscles are recovering from heavy exercises and you need a break, you can practice these exercises to utilize that time because they do not hinder muscle recovery. A balanced body can unconsciously understand its center of gravity. So, do not undermine the power of balance exercises, as they set the base for high-intensity sports like boxing and running, making your body and mind stable and sharp.

Let's discuss of you examples of balance exercises:

- Tightrope walk: Remember we discussed walking on a line of bricks? There are people in the world who are able to walk on hanging ropes. You can use the same exercise at a moderate level to increase your balance at home. Place a long string in front of you in a straight line and start at one end. Take slow but steady steps ahead, placing one foot exactly in front of the other and making sure your feet do not fall out of the line. Take at least 15 such steps ahead and start walking in reverse in the same manner. Once you get used to this, try the edge of a pavement outdoors.

- Flamingo stand: Stand straight with your feet together. Fold and lift one leg as high as you can and put it back in place. Repeat with the other leg. If your balance is already in place, you can start doing this fast to turn this into a cardio exercise called high knees. Maintain a straight posture at all times and keep your tummy tucked in. For the next level of difficulty, after you reach your foot up, snuggle it close to your chest and hold it in place for 15 seconds. Repeat with the other. For an even more difficult version, spread your arms like a bird on both sides and hold the folded knee as high as you can without providing hand support. You can also try any of these with your eyes closed for even better effects.

- Standing weight shift: Stand with both your feet with a gap of one shoulder. Start with distributing weight between both your feet. Now, shift your weight to one side and lift the other foot straight to the respective side. Raise as high as possible without leaving your straight posture. Repeat on the other side.

- Heel lift: Stand straight on a yoga mat and lift your heels as you shift the weight of your body to the toes. Hold for a few seconds. Keep repeating this in a pattern. When you get better at this, you can try walking on your toes without falling.

- Tree pose: Stand straight on a yoga mat with your hands straight up and pressed together with your palms facing each other. Breathe deeply, raise one leg, and fold it. Place the sole of your foot on the inner thigh of the other leg, pulling the folded foot as high up as you can. Initially, you can start by placing the sole lower, near the ankle.

- Mountain pose: The next pose will probably surprise you as it sounds like you are just standing straight. So, stand straight on a yoga mat, but make sure your feet are very closely stuck together. Now, look straight and raise your hands above your head to bring them together in the *Namaskara* position or a clapping position, where the palms are stuck together. Now, correct your posture perfectly. Lower your shoulders and push them backward, push your chest in front, tuck your tummy in, and pull yourself up as if gravity is pulling you in reverse.

Stand in this position for 15–20 seconds. It is more difficult than it sounds to balance with your feet together.

- Bird-dog pose: Get to a tabletop position on the yoga mat with your palms, knees, and toes touching the ground and your back parallel to the ground. Let the right hand in front of you, and with the left leg behind you, make a straight line parallel to the ground. Hold for 10–15 seconds as you look forward. Repeat on the other side. You can also bring the knee and the elbow to touch each other under your trunk in the same tabletop position after a set on each side; hold again for a few seconds.

- Tiger pose: In the continuity of the last position, fold your leg behind from the foot and push it upward. Hold like this with both hands on the ground in the tabletop position. Once you can manage this, reach the foot with the tip of the other hand and hold the toe. Look straight and hold till you can. Repeat on the other side.

The world of workouts is relatively new to me, also. I recently discovered the joy of being able to rejuvenate my body parts with physical activities. It feels so much more fresh every morning when I wake up. I had started to lose a lot of skills in the body as well as the mind with age, but I was accepting them as normal like most people do. Now, it is like I entered a new-found world and can't be happier for having stumbled upon this door.

Do you know that most of the diseases we take as acceptable are actually not? The reality is that you do not need to live with frozen shoulders, bad posture, back pain, sleep disorders, high blood sugar and blood pressure, weak lungs and heart, and many other diseases that you thought were just a part of life. Wake up because it is not too late. Whenever you wake up in the morning, let's take a pledge today to make our body a better place to live in because this is a permanent home for you and me that can never be changed—only treated, healed, and exited one day.

Now that we have talked about so many physical diseases, it is also important to come to the discussion of mental well-being, which might not be as visible but is as crucial to treat and cater to. Mental and physical well-being are very closely knit together and interdependent. Let us understand more in the next chapter.

Chapter 5:

Nurturing Your Mind Palace

The health of a person is a broad spectrum. Apart from their organs, veins, bones, and other parts of the body working functionally, their social relations, personal feelings, and spiritual upliftment also have a crucial role to play when they define how they are doing overall. But one element that we often tend to miss out on is mental health. Out of the 300,000 years of our species Homo Sapiens on the face of this Earth and the 50–65,000 years of their modern-day versions, medics and doctors for treating physical ailments have been present for at least 5,000 years. Now, guess how many thousands of years mental health practitioners have been around for. Any guesses? About 100. That's right.

The mind is one of the oldest things on the planet, and its recognition as something to be looked after is as recent as a century. Some psychiatric professionals raised a flag for human rights as recently as 1908 to improve the quality of mental health. This movement was called The Mental Hygiene Movement, and it started the journey of recognition and treatment of mental health as it is today. When a person faces mental health issues, sometimes they might bring the roof down, and some other times they might be as silent as a grey day in London. However, the impact of such issues and diseases can change the lives of individuals and families. The most dangerous thing about mental health issues is not the issues but the lack of recognition. Most planet-dwellers *still* think that treating your mental issues will make you a *lunatic* and that psychiatrists and counselors are doctors for mad people. There is a severe lack of awareness in terms of the ailments and their symptoms and an unimaginable social stigma about accepting them. While our awareness has gone up over time, mental health issues are also becoming more common by the day, given our pace and complications of life. They lead to substance abuse, physical and mental abuse of self and others, compromised social identity and personal relationships, and deteriorated quality of life.

Think of an iceberg when you see it from afar. If you see a huge triangle above the level of water, that is but the tip of the iceberg. When you see symptoms of mental health issues, it is usually a small fragment of the actual issue. The heavier and darker secrets are always hidden underwater which can only be excavated.

The Importance of Mental Health

When a person is happy and in a healthy state of mind, they can enjoy life, manage stress, and maintain relationships with positivity. When mental health is in place, your physical health is automatically better. With lower levels of stress, your immune system is sounder, helping you fight diseases and stay healthier. Your blood sugar and pressure levels can be controlled with mental fitness, and the release of happy hormones—which we read about in the section for exercise—can keep your body chemically healthier.

When you are mentally fit and well, you feel more productive and develop the willingness to contribute to society, whether at your workplace, your community, or when you are alone. Healthy individuals tend to be engaged and involved in the work they do, positively contribute to gaining further validation from there, and focus on achieving their goals. When you are mentally fit, you naturally deal with the challenges life throws at you with more ease and confidence. You develop the endurance and resilience to think, *I have handled this before, and I can handle it again.* Resilient people can bounce back easily, get back on track, and make lemonades out of the lemons that life gifts.

When other people, their moments, expectations, and your relationships with them. A happier person will tend to be more patient when listening to another person, even if they are ranting and just need to be heard. To handle another person's vulnerability, you need to be strong yourself, and that strength can only come when you are mentally in control. If you keep unhappy, dissatisfied, and unfulfilled in your own head, you will find it difficult to wear another person's shoes and look at the world through their eyes. This will lead to never-ending disputes, lower chances of reconciliation, and strained relationships, causing gradual isolation and further damage to mental health. When you are mentally unhealthy, handling your emotions like stress, anger, jealousy, disbelief, distrust, and so on can also feel difficult, thus keeping you and your near and dear ones unhappy. You might end up behaving in ways you do not want to. Emotional well-being greatly depends upon mental health.

When more humans are mentally healthy, society and the community tend to grow into compassionate empaths who can support each other. Just like a pandemic as deadly as COVID-19 that took the world by storm and changed a few generations, as humans, mental health issues can sweep people off their base without really showing signs till the damage has eaten up from within like termites. A healthy population can make a better tomorrow. When people stop performing lower, decreased productivity, excessive funds drainage in healthcare, and lower interest in social and community services can lead to major economic consequences. If mental healthcare can be prioritized from the beginning, these burdens can be reduced.

Finally, a mentally healthy person feels happy and fulfilled and is more inclined to reach the point of self-actualization. Remember the Maslow's pyramid of hierarchy? The tip of the pyramid talks about the final purpose for the human mind to find a sense of purpose and meaning for living life. This point of ultimate personal fulfillment can only be achieved with consistent and steadily positive mental health.

Now that we have discussed so much about why mental health should be balanced, let us also think about how to do it better.

Work Out Your Mind

Keep your mind at work at all times except for when you sleep. A tired body and a tired mind can get good rest and deep sleep in the night. By tired, I mean working but not stressed. Remember how we discussed the importance of workouts to tire your body out before bedtime and hence put you to sleep easily and enough? Similarly, if your mind is at work when you are awake, you can increase the sharpness of your brain and make it more functional, rest better, and hence be more productive in your daily life. This is what the name of the book suggests—*The Six-Pack Mind*. Strength exercises for the six-pack mind include mind games. Here are a few you can try:

- Play a jigsaw puzzle. Start with pictures made by joining bigger pieces and gradually work your way toward smaller pieces. The smaller the pieces, the longer it takes and the more your brain works out.

- Play card games like solitaire, bridge, and poker and board games like chess to keep your mind active at all times and put all your senses at work while calculating, watching, and observing. Your memory and your skills for quick-thinking can be improved greatly by such games.

- Improve your linguistic sense by carrying a notebook and a pen with you or keeping notes open on your phone. Whenever you hear or read a new word, write it down along with the meaning so that you can read the list later and increase your vocabulary.

- Learning to dance, play an instrument, or a new language can sharpen your brain so that your mind is made to remember the moves, chords, tones, or alphabets and words. This increases your memory and capacity to retain relevant information.

- Sit at a particular place and look around using all your senses. If you are at a park, smell everything you find from petrichor to a woman's perfume, hear everything from the vibrations of crickets to thunders in clouds, taste everything from ice cream to the salty taste of the air, touch anything from a cold bench to water in the sea, and see everything from grass to the people walking around. Practice using all your senses.

- Learn new skills at home, in the community, or at work, and teach such skills to others. Learning and transferring the knowledge makes your own learning foolproof.

- Whether you are driving, cycling, walking to work, or even taking a bus or the subway, try different routes to reach the same place to test your cognitive and analytical skills.

- Sit at a place and do a full body scan. Close your eyes and focus on one part of your body at a time. Start from the tip of your toe through your full body and end at the crown of your head.

Let us now get into details and find a few habits for the mind that can make life better in this chapter. These are easy entries in your schedule and thought process and won't take a huge effort to incorporate.

Positive Thoughts

When you use high-quality materials to make a house, your building is stronger, weatherproof, and safe. When you use positive thoughts as a base for all other ideas, the ideas are concrete and sensible. A negative mind is the perfect oven to bake bad plans, take wrong calls, and make wrong decisions. When you start to think positively, you will see wonders happen. Positive thoughts attract positive events in life. When you think positive, you are confident. You start to believe in yourself and have more faith in others. You know the outcome will be good and hence feel motivated to work for it. Positive thoughts can empower your mind and make you believe that you cracked that interview, bagged that job, won that heart, started afresh, ran that marathon, learned to drive, spoke that language, forgave that friend, and so on. Situations could be different every day, but a base of strong and assertive thoughts can take you a long way.

When you think positive, you can also put more trust in others. With positive thoughts, you will try to understand why people behave a certain way and look at things from beyond your own perspective. Your relationships are bound to evolve better that way. Every time you face a negative situation, a positive mind will think solution-oriented rather than crib over the issue. Positive thoughts will keep you chemically balanced.

The hormones you secrete inside will be happy hormones and the emotions you will experience perenially are joy, fulfillment, contentment, and gratitude toward the things you have and not regret and envy about the things you don't. Positivity makes you feel safe about the basic requirements in life and thus lets your mind wander into the realms of imagination. This helps you solve problems creatively and bring innovation into life and work.

Build Trust

Because of low moral values and lack of importance ascribed to keeping promises in the modern world, trust issues develop in most of us. It is important to fight against the instinct for our own well-being and promote a positive environment of mutual trust in the air. When people get hurt once, and especially if they leave a trauma, the hypothalamus area of the brain overreacts to the simplest of situations and complicates them. The hypothalamus is the link in the brain between the endocrine and nervous system. Its main job is to keep your brain in a balanced state, which is called homeostasis. It is also the organ that is supposed to protect your brain from getting hurt. It alerts you in danger so that you can brace yourself.

During the times of the hunters and gatherers, if a predator was around, the hypothalamus would immediately alert our ancestors, asking them to go to a safe place to protect themselves. A situation where we get scared of some harm is called a fight-or-flight situation, where we either retaliate by giving it a fight or our brain tells us it is too dangerous and asks us to take a flight from the scene. The hypothalamus is the control coordination system of the brain and does not know when the fight-or-flight mode needs to be switched off. Because it knows that you have been hurt in a similar situation sometime long back, it might ask you to raise your guard in unnecessary situations where you don't need to freak out. This promotes distrust and takes away from your mental peace. If you keep distrusting yourself and others, it will hamper both your confidence and relationships.

Self-Counseling and Chatting With Self

The truth also remains that most people are too busy in their lives and do not find a strong support system. In that case, also, it is the best thing if you can fall back on yourself.

Spend some time with yourself every day, preferably at the same time of the day as a part of your routine, and find out where you stand. Talk to yourself about your victories and failures, friends and adversaries, favorites and bêtes noires, morning coffees and evening drinks, good habits and bad, deep sleep and insomnia, work and passion, plans and surprises, etc. Remember how certain situations and people make you feel now versus in the past.

If you keep talking to yourself with concentration and ascribe value to this conversation, you can soon get used to this and will probably start loving it. It is a healthy habit that helps you analyze situations and make the right decisions, relieving stress by confiding in the most nonjudgmental space, rehearsing for speeches and presentations before facing the actual audience, processing difficult or new information, and accompanying yourself if you suffer from loneliness. Most importantly, conversations with the self promote self-awareness, which is the first step to solving most problems in life.

Meditation

A controlled mind is the strongest mind. Swami Vivekananda, the celebrated Indian author and philosopher, compared the human mind to a turbulent monkey who goes berserk when the chain of emotions like desire, achievements and failures, jealousy, and pride parade in the head (Vivekananda, 1896).

Now imagine the world being a zoo full of monkeys running around and creating chaos brainlessly. What would come of such a world? Nothing but devastation. To bring your thoughts and mind in control, you need to practice daily. Just like regular practice can make you good at math, the right exercises can also help you control your head.

Play some peaceful music, relax your head, close your eyes, and meditate. Filling your head with a vacuum sounds easier than done. Meditation is to replace your existing chaotic thoughts with planned, organized, and streamlined thoughts. Meditation can help you grow your attention, feel relaxed, and also achieve elevated awareness. Different kinds of meditation include breathing exercises, body scans, grounding exercises, and others. In addition, you can chant a bunch of mantras or words that give out positive vibrations or listen to their recorded versions and gather your focus in place. If none of the means are available or possible, you can simply stare at one point in front of you and focus there, ruling out all sounds and sights around you.

Breathing Techniques

- Take a deep breath for four seconds, hold the breath for four more seconds, and release the breath again for four seconds. This pattern is called box breathing.

- Sit straight and inhale for two seconds. Pout your lips like you are about to whistle. Breathe out through your lips for four seconds. This is called pursed breathing.

- Sit straight and cover your right nostril with your thumb as you breathe in from your left nostril. Now, use your ring finger and little finger to cover your left nostril as you breathe out from your right nostril. In the next round, you can do the same thing on the other side. This is called alternate nostril breathing.

- If you do not want to exercise your breath in a certain way or limit it to timings and patterns, this one is perfect for you. Keep breathing normally, and focus and notice how you are breathing with closed eyes. When your mind wanders off, go and bring it back to the breath like you would bring back a naughty child. This is called mindfulness breathing.

These are patterns you can repeat as many times as you need in times of anxiety and restlessness. Moreover, you can practice them daily for long-term improvement of nerves and concentration. Sit upright with your chest pushed in front, your arms resting on your thighs, and your shoulders relaxed. When breathing in, fill your lungs with air and inflate your stomach. Hold this position as long as you keep your breath held. Deflate your stomach like a pricked balloon as you exhale.

Grounding Exercises

Grounding basically means living in the moment and focusing on it. You can ground yourself simply by sitting in one place and minutely noticing everything happening around you, like cars moving, birds chirping, raindrops falling, and even a clock ticking. Standing under the shower and feeling water bouncing off your head is also grounding. My favorite grounding exercises are walking on the grass or hugging a huge tree trunk. Coming close to nature reminds me of our roots and the very core of life. Besides, you can sit on the grass when you have time, close your eyes, and imagine your body as the trunk of a tree. You can then try thinking of your roots penetrating the soil underneath and your branches growing upward to touch the sky.

Escape Routes and Safe Spaces

No matter how strong and resilient we become, we all try to look for a place to run and hide when negative emotions take over. Guess what. You can create that space for yourself, even in your head. One way to do it would be to create a physical space, like decorating a corner of the house to your own liking and stacking it with your favorite things like a cushion, a guitar, some books, etc. But inside your head, there are no limitations to your safe space. You can paint any picture you like without having to consider the practicalities of budget, location, and possibilities. For instance, you can create a neon sparkling ocean on the bosom of a different planet with glowing starfish on the sea bed. You can place your favorite armchair right at the beach and surround yourself with your favorite people, living or dead, to create a space you would want to stay at. Your imagination is your biggest strength here.

Expressing Through Art

If you have been an artist as a child or when you were younger, the easiest way to escape your worries would be to go back there again. Pick up that paintbrush, strum through those strings of that guitar, make your bachata moves, or just start writing the novel you have always dreamt of. There is no better escape route than art to forget your worries and create a parallel world where you can keep yourself happy and positively engaged.

And what if you have never considered yourself an artist? Well, the good news is that art is not limited to *artists*. There are several videos available on YouTube today for DIY home crafts. Take a Random glass jar, wrap it with colorful paper and ribbons, and make a Christmas decor. Cut old bedsheets into half if you are tired of seeing them on your bed, stitch them up with other fabric, and make them into curtains or table runners. Give your house a new look with little shifts in the furniture at the weekend. You can simply head to the kitchen with a colorful salad using a recipe you have never used before, and that, too, can count for art.

You can use your imagination to do your own nail art, scribble on paper and make a doodle, cut colorful paper into small pieces, make wall art, and much more.

Basically, any activity you do with your creative imagination and skills can be called art as long as it invokes certain emotions in you, even if the world does not understand them or approve of them.

Chakra Healing

Chakras but are said to be controlling the primal functions of the body, soul, and mind." They literally mean disc or wheel. They originate from major Eastern traditions but have made a very important place in new-age spirituality. The root chakra, or the muladhar chakra, is located at the end of the spine and is related to survival instincts and human beings' sense of security. The sacral, or swadhishthana chakra, is located in the lower abdomen and relates to emotional balance, sexuality, and creativity. The third chakra is the solar plexus, or manipura chakra, located in the upper abdomen, and it empowers you with self-esteem and confidence. The heart, or anahata chakra, is located in the middle of the chest and governs emotional well-being, including love and compassion. The throat, or vishuddha chakra, is placed in the throat area as the name suggests, and dominates a person's skills of communication and self-expression. The third eye, or ajna chakra, is found between the two eyebrows and relates to a person's perception, intuition, and spiritual awakening. The last chakra commonly talked about is the crown chakra, or sahasara chakra, located at the crown of the head and associated with the connection to spirituality and higher powers.

While none of these wheels are physical organs, great minds have agreed that their existence and attunement can impact human life very strongly. There are multiple processes to follow in order to balance your chakras, most of which have been discussed in this book. Balancing your chakras can bring you peace, prosperity, health, wealth, and all that you seek.

Journaling Your Thoughts

As we discussed before, it is very important to have regular talks with yourself. But sometimes, verbal expression is not enough.

Journaling can help you list the number of things you are grateful for in a day or in the long run. It can help you set goals and keep a physical account of them so that you can remind yourself of your progress, congratulate yourself for the goals achieved, and push yourself to work toward what remains unachieved. By writing in full sentences, you can improve your linguistic proficiency and expression skills. You can also use your journal to track your personal growth and shift your perspective about different events, people, and happenings around you. You can express freely in a nonjudgmental zone the way you cannot in front of anybody in this world. Journaling, especially with printouts of pictures or soft copies in case you are typing, can act as a personal record of memories of your lifetime which you can go back to later in life for a good laugh or a teary moment.

Apart from being your instrument for self-reflection and outlet for emotions, journaling can help you write your problems with probable solutions, write the probable outcomes for each one of them, and gradually strike out the wrong options to be left with the right thing to do.

Over and above everything, leaving aside all agendas and journaling can help you manage your stress better and leave you a little happier every time you finish.

Support Groups and Support Systems

Your support system is the biggest resource you can have. As you grow older and wiser, you will understand that a handful of supportive and understanding humans is far more precious than a flock of people to hang out and drink with. When you face a problem in life, a heartbreak that keeps you awake, a physical ailment that limits your mobility, a mental health issue like social anxiety, or simply the need to be heard, these people are what you need at your disposal. We will learn more about how to maintain such relations in the next chapter.

These people need not be related by blood but by love and compassion. Apart from friends, family, neighbors, and acquaintances, you can join groups and communities to do your favorite things with them, like a book reading club, a hiking club, or a Zumba class to meet new people, a few of whom might end up being your closest people later on in the walk of life. To get the support you want, you need to learn how to extend a similar hand of support to others.

Beyond creating a natural habitat of supporting cast for the movie of your life, you can also opt for tailor-made support groups. Find groups around you where many people like you come together and share their experiences to make you feel better and just one in a group of people instead of feeling lonely. For instance, an alcoholic might go to rehab for a few months, the tenure of which will depend upon the intensity of their addiction. At the rehab, there will be many others who have gone through different traumas in life which might have gotten them addicted to various substances. Some of those people will have come out of the vicious cycle better than them and end up inspiring them for a better and liberated future. Some others might be in a worse shape and the alcoholic who has been sidelined at most social gatherings till now will now have found a place to feel like the bigger person and inspire someone else instead. This makes one realize the futility of complaining about their own situation and focusing on genuine attempts instead. Whenever life feels drab and hopeless, these are the people they can reach out to and remind themselves of the better things in life.

Pursuing a Hobby

Allow yourself a particular time slot every day before or after your daily chores and work, and try to stick to that. If you can manage to sit with it only at the weekends, that's okay, too, but incorporating this activity into your schedule is important. Creating a particular physical space to sit and work on your hobby can increase your concentration and instruct your mind for the activity automatically. Once you find yourself interested, invest gradually in the equipment and tools you may need to pursue your activity. Unless you find the possibility of a long-term commitment, do not end up investing too much money lest it gets wasted. If engaging all alone seems like a laborious task, join a community where other people engage in the same activity, provide their insights, value yours, encourage each other, and give you a sense of belongingness.

If you have started and need to get better at your hobby, join a regular class or go for short-term workshops offline or online as per your choice. These classes can take your skill a notch higher and win you a mentor who might choose to help you later when you get stuck. Patience and persistence are two important skills to acquire, as we discussed under the system of the 4 Ps. While you might be doing well at your hobby, remember there is always scope for improvement, and practice will get you there.

When you know the basics, explore further and figure out the new things you can do with your skills. Finally, even though timelines and set goals are important, don't forget the importance of enjoying what you are doing since that is the point of a hobby anyway. Balance out expectations and enjoyment in a way that you develop and cultivate yourself and also feel good about what you do.

Clean, Dust, and Maintain Your Mind Palace

Like your house needs regular cleaning, decorating, and maintenance, your mind palace needs all of that and more.

Clean negative thoughts with the duster of positivity exercises, decorate the shelves of your head with little things that appeal to you and make you look good in front of the world, and maintain the balance, focus, and calmness of your mind with regular practice and mindfulness.

If you are conscious of your thoughts and actions, half your job toward achieving a balanced mindset and behavioral pattern is done. Stay fit and happy, make healthy choices every day, and respect yourself as much as other people. And life shall be good. One very important trick to react with calmness in a turbulent situation is to hold your breath, count to 10, and use this time to ask yourself if your instinctive reaction will solve the situation or make it worse. If you wait it out and then react instead of lashing out, you will most probably make the right decision and respond responsibly rather than react impulsively. I will share several other tips to develop good habits and take your mind and body in control with you in the next chapter. So stay tuned and stay well. Until next time, then!

Chapter 6:

Lessons for Life That No One Told You About

Your life is yours. You can make or break it as you go through the journey of life. When I was young, I used to listen to this song called "Que Sera Sera," where a woman grows up asking different people in her life, like her mother and her lover, about the possibilities of the future. They tell her, "Que Sera Sera, Whatever will be, will be, The future's not ours to see..." (Day, 2008).

She says the same to her children when they ask her about the future.

Uncertainty is the only certainty that we know of about the future. You don't know today if the party you are so excited to go to tomorrow will even happen. You can plan to visit your parents next year, but you don't know if they will live to see the day next year. You plan to eat Chinese for dinner, but you don't know if the Chinese eatery at the corner of the street will be open tonight. But amidst all this uncertainty, do you leave everything to fate? I do believe in destiny. Whatever will be, will probably be. But if I am here in this world and can move my brain and body parts around to contribute to my future, then I might as well, right?

Even if you can't dictate your life completely, it is your thoughts and actions that contribute to it or set the direction, at the least. So, the next time you curse your fate for making you pay for the things you never did, think twice. Did you contribute to the outcomes of your life? Let's discuss some basics of life, in general, that can help you know yourself and the world better, develop good habits, and know the right things to say and do.

Time and Money on Your Balancing Scale

So, colorman, colorman, which color do you choose? Do you spend your time doing the things you love and spending with the people you love, or do you spend your time running after earning money? The answer is this and that.

Before you think I will romanticize time and passion, here is a reality check. Money is very, very important. Doing what you like and following your passion is all great, but unless you are born with a silver spoon in your mouth that is dependable and you are also comfortable with living off someone else's money, you need to figure out how to make money. The basics need to be in place for all of us. I am referring to Maslow's theory again. Unless you have food, water, clean clothes, and a secure home, following your passion, spending time with dear ones, and anything above those two levels of the pyramid are not your priority. Making money is important, and saving it for the future is even more important.

On the other hand, money can be made in a day if you are lucky and lost in seconds if you are not. But time can neither be bought and sold nor brought back and extended. The laziest of people who spend their time doing nothing might win the lottery in one evening and become rich, but not even the richest of people can go back in time and bring back their childhood or dead parents. The thing is, time is the precious gift of the almighty Universe that never stands still, and money is just a currency made by mere mortals for transactional exchange. So, when you gift someone your time, it is the resource that will never come back. This moment you are spending to read my lines will never come back to you in your lifetime.

What is the answer then? Is time more important? Should we use our time doing only the things we love? Here is the thing. This choice is personal. Some people prefer earning a lot of money to create a safety net for themselves and then earn even more for the next generations and their own luxury. Others might want to only earn what they need and rather spend their time happily with their family, friends, and other sources of happiness. When you educate yourself and know how to let your money grow even when you are sleeping, you have more time in your hands to spend doing whatever you please. So, the moral of the story is that to understand how to crack this balance, you need to understand yourself and your priorities better, which takes us back to the earlier chapters. Whether you will be happier doing a swanky job far away from your family or you will feel fulfilled holding your parents' hands when they need you, even if that means less money, no one will know but you.

Response and Reaction

As humans, we are all slaves of our impulses. When someone slaps us, we want to slap them back or hurt exactly where it hurts the most. When a long-time intense relationship ends, we feel like getting into a rebound with the next person that we go out with. When we feel like eating a dessert, we want to order immediately. When there is a difficult situation at work, we want to send in a resignation letter immediately.

Now you are thinking, Trevor does not want me to stand up for myself. Well, hear me out. All I am saying is, in any given situation, instead of reacting on the face of the matter, what if you take a breath, wait a moment, analyze the situation, and make a conscious decision about your retaliation? My grandmother used to say, "Never respond to a negative comment, especially with anger and spite in the room. It is always more sensible to wait it out and come back with a well-thought-out answer after a gap."

Let's take the examples of Mr. Impulse and Mrs. Impulse, who have been living together for the past seven years. They care for each other deeply and have stood by each other through difficult times. Yet, the fact remains that they are very different as individuals. The man likes to keep everything in the house organized to the T, and the lady likes to clean up all at once at the weekend. Mr. Impulse says that he enjoys coming back to a clean home and easily finds his things when they are left in their right places. Mrs. Impulse says she feels tired after work and cooking and hence prefers cleaning and organizing for the weekend when she can do it all with a clear head. This is a recurring problem that gives rise to regular fights. One evening, Mrs. Impulse went too far and told her husband that he was a patient with OCD like his dead mother. Bringing his mother into the picture hurt Mr. Impulse very much and he retaliated, saying that she was only a clerk and did not work as hard as him at the office. She then said that it was for the family that she couldn't take up promotions and that she was tired of working *like a maid* for him at home. He instantly asked her to stop *sacrificing her life* for him and get a divorce. She was shocked at his statement and packed her bags to leave home. Phew! What started with simple decisions about when to clean the house took them to court in no time. Touching these topics was never a part of the plan for either but the hotheaded tiff brought them there. An ocean of tears and a battle of piercing arrows were witnessed at the house, which broke down like a house of cards.

When things get out of hand, having a conversation and a discussion with the mindset of understanding each other can take you a long way. During fights, our emotions get the better of us, and we end up saying a lot of things that we do not mean to. The goal should be to control your mind in a way that you can overcome the impulse to hurt the person in front of you and rather take a solution-oriented approach. Even though Mrs. Impulse had passed a comment he did not like, Mr. Impulse could have just tried telling her instead that she was crossing the line talking about his dead mother and how much that hurt him.

It is, hence, extremely important to know how to respond to a situation with the help of instinct and thoughts rather than react immediately at impulse.

To do this properly, you need to get a hang of communication skills and learn how to provide as well as accept constructive feedback even when it is negative. There is hardly any problem in the world that communication cannot solve.

Here are a few main points to remember for effective communication:

- Listen carefully to know what the other person said exactly, and try to understand the difference between their words and their meaning, if any. Listening is the first step for communicating and the only way a conversation can go in the right direction.

- Make sure to convey your ideas and statements in a loud and clear voice but also in a tone that is respectful and non-condescending. Use proper sentences and the right expressions to fill the communication gaps. Be assertive, not vague.

- Be very conscious of your nonverbal expressions, like body language, gestures, and facial expressions. They add to a conversation equally, if not more than verbal expressions.

- When talking to someone you care for, try to keep your ego aside and be open to receiving negative feedback. When giving negative feedback, try to be explanatory and not harsh in your approach. The idea is to convey why you are hurt and not how much at fault the other is.

- Ask yourself if your reaction will only make you feel relieved of your stress or contribute anything toward solving the real problem. Go ahead with the reaction only if the latter stands true. Otherwise, think of a different approach.

- Being too aggressive can scare the other person or shut them up, and being way too passive can allow the other person to walk over you. None of these is the right thing to do. Find a balance between passive and aggressive so that you can both put your point forward clearly and listen to the other person with an open heart.

- Finally, no matter how difficult the conversation is, respect yourself and the other. The conversation and the problem will end sometime, but it must not cost you your relationship.

Be Who You Look Up To

We have always had heroes in childhood we looked up to. As we grow older, we realize we have the potential to become those heroes. I believe in admiring people who inspire me and identifying the traits in them that appeal to me. Then, I try to imbibe those qualities in my own life. Qualities don't sit in people just like that. Little changes in lifestyle and acquiring little habits can bring magic into your life. Trust me, it is the little changes in your everyday schedule that make the real difference.

A few years back, I made a decision to take things up into my own hands rather than sulking about the things that kept going wrong and I kept cribbing, "Why me?" Turns out, the Universe has everything in abundance for all of us. It is on us to catch the better things and release the worse. As I said in the beginning, I am no spiritual guide or life coach. I can tell you what I did and what worked best. Here are a few things that might help. Thank me later!

- Let us start with the beginning of the day. Going to bed early and waking up early is unparalleled as a habit. When you sleep at 2 a.m., even if you sleep for 8 hours, it can not give you as much rest as sleeping at 10 p.m. for 6 hours would give. Go to sleep like a baby and wake up fresh and rejuvenated. If you can wake up before the sun and witness the beginning of the day, that is the best way to begin your day.

- While it is the best idea to get a compact night's sleep for 6–8 hours, it is okay to take a power nap during the early afternoon between 1 p.m.

and 3 p.m. if paired with proper exercise. Seniors especially might need a little daytime sleep to keep up with the second half of the day.

- Brush your teeth, clean your face, wear fresh and loose clothes, and spray a body mist if you like. Make your bed every day and sleep on a clean sheet. Importantly, finish dinner a few hours before bedtime and go for a brisk walk afterward.

- Keep away from habits like smoking and drinking because you never know which puff or sip will be your last. I believe in enjoying life and doing what you love once in a while, but don't let your bad habits enslave you. Keep them leashed instead.

- Start your day with a stretch and meditation, or spend some me-time on the balcony with a cup of steaming black coffee if you so prefer. Many researchers do not recommend having tea or coffee on an empty stomach. You can rather make several kinds of detox water to sip on in the morning and during the day to regularize your blood pressure and sugar levels and purify your blood.

- Exercise, yoga, a brisk walk, or a run are all good habits to start your day. A round of physical activity will pump you up and enliven the rest of the day.

- Maintain your personal hygiene and take it very seriously. Keep a tab of when you shave, comb, shampoo, etc. It will keep you safe from infections and diseases, keep you feeling and looking better, and trust me, your date will appreciate it!

- Eat what you make in the kitchen. The preservatives in food items that can be left for months are killing you slowly but steadily. Mood food additives to extend the life of a packaged food product are shown to lead to long-term diseases like irritability, headache, cardiovascular diseases, asthma, and even cancer. Instead of buying packed and sliced bread, for example, bake your own or make a bowl of porridge for breakfast. Instead of buying canned juice, juice your fruits, or even better, eat them whole to get all the richness of the *fibers*.

- Include fibers, protein, leaves, and nuts in your diet, and make a balanced diet chart to follow every day. Clip it to the door of your fridge to guide you.

- If you have an unhealthy eating pattern where junk food and a lot of high-fat and sweet food make their way onto your plate, the only answer is to learn to say no. I promise you that once you discard them, walk a healthy road, and see the benefits for yourself, you will not want to eat them again.

- You might have heard a lot of people say that sugar is good for you and gives you energy. Well, they are wrong. The glucose your body needs for a supply of energy comes from natural sugar, which is broadly categorized as fructose, which comes from fruits, and lactose, which comes from milk and milk products. Added sugar is the sugar you add to your coffee, cereals, or desserts for the kick of sugary food, and that is in no way good for your body.

- Exercise every day and follow the tips I added in Chapter 4. Running and cycling are basic cardio exercises to keep you in shape and pump blood to your heart, but adding balance and strength exercises to your regime has its own set of benefits, which we have discussed before.

- Keep a positive mindset and journal your reasons for gratitude and list of goals and dreams every day. Do this at a fixed time every day and use this book as an account of your life.

- Use small windows of your time to clean little sections of the house regularly and utilize holidays and weekends to do the deep cleaning work. Cleaning is also best done in the morning after workouts so that you can enjoy the rest of your resting day in peace.

- Set deadlines for the bigger as well as smaller goals. Keep a note of your work goals and tick them off when done. Similarly, keep a note of things you need to do for yourself and your home, and make sure to have deadlines against them.

- All work and no play makes John a dull boy. Consider yourself John and make sure to pull out some time for your favorite things like watching movies, catching up with friends, playing an instrument, or even lazing around doing nothing. We all have our own ways of coping with the race called life, and we deserve to take that time out.

- Cap your time for looking at the screen and keep your phone away for at least an hour before hitting the bed. Resting your eyes is very important, and staring at strange things on social media before bed affects your sleep and dreams.

- Finally, lead a conscious life and be a mindful person. Read a lot and gather knowledge about the things you see, eat, do, hear, and breathe. When you know yourself and your environment well, you will be in a position to decide what is what. Living a mindful life will solve most of your problems, and for the rest, you need to know how to cope and start again.

Working on Human Relations

"I don't need anyone" is easier said than done. For thousands of centuries, we have been wired to live with a community of people. These communities that used to eat, sleep, hunt, and party together started to break down into smaller groups. From forming bands of people to living in large joint families took thousands of years, but the journey from joint families to nuclear families and now to individuals living alone was a short one. We are quickly becoming solitary and lonely animals while we were fabricated to be social animals. The fulfillment that comes from living in harmony with people will not be attained if you try to form a self-sustaining cocoon where you live alone. There are individualistic animals in the animal kingdom, but we are not some of them.

You need to be in touch with your partner, friends, family, community, and society at large. The relationship changes and shifts the paradigm with every person you deal with. Maintaining connections with other humans involves conscious efforts and in the right direction. Humans are not preset machines. Every one of them behaves differently from the other and even the behavior of the same person will be different in different situations.

The first thing to remember is that everyone around is looking for a patient ear. Giving them a place to vent out and talk to when they need it is the biggest way to show someone that you care. Understand when to respond and when to listen quietly. If you don't have anything to console or advice, just listen while providing them warmth. You can do that with your body language—nodding, placing a hand on their shoulder, maintaining eye contact to show involvement and presence... depending on the comfort of physical closeness. If you have a suggestion and you think it might hurt them, be very wary about how to put it across. Before giving negative feedback, always try to cushion it with some positive words of affirmation and appreciation first.

To understand how they feel, first try to understand who they are and what they have gone through. Try to put yourself in their shoes to get a better perspective of their complaints. For instance, a six-year-old child often refers to their earlier events as *childhood*. You will obviously find this funny because the child is still very young, but from their point of view, three years of age is just half of the time they have been alive. Their little problems, like doing their homework or eating broccoli are big from their perspective. Similarly, if your wife, mother, or sister, who is a homemaker and never really left the confines of her house, treats little things in the outside world too seriously, you need to look at the world from inside the house and not from your office desk. This will help you be empathetic toward the person you talk to and make them comfortable in sharing their problem.

Work on your communication skills—the way you construct your sentences, build up a conversation, and express through bodily gestures and facial expressions. Communicating comes with the responsibility of conveying what you mean and not something else. Also, one great thing about effective communication is that you need to remember how the person wants to hear it besides how you want to say it if you care for the receiver.

Even though we talk about being ourselves and choosing to behave how we want to with our dear people, in reality, courtesy and respect need to be maintained with anyone you deal with. Not just your parents or colleagues but your friends and children, too, will expect respect when you talk to them. You can only demand respect when you emit it. If you are dealing with people from a different cultural, geographical, or religious background, remember to value their opinions, keeping in mind that they might not match yours owing to the difference in backgrounds and upbringing. If you don't know about their opinions and thoughts and why they are shaped like that, you can ask them and have a heart-to-heart conversation. If conflicts arise, try to resolve them peacefully by looking for common grounds and solutions that can affect both parties positively. Being transparent does not mean being rude. The same thing can be said in a hundred ways, and just the choice of words and way of speaking make a huge difference. Remember to make promises only when you can fulfill them because that builds trust and reliability, two markers for a respectable entity.

For professional relations, attend seminars and events, join professional groups, network with people from your field, and actively participate in conversations with a keen interest.

Appreciate others, including your subordinates and your partner, and don't hesitate to do that publicly. Recognize their efforts and positive inputs and try to overlook the negatives as long as they do not affect your life deeply. Value other people's time and your own. Reach at dates and parties on time and also work meetings.

While you keep your loved ones and other good people close and comforted, also remember to scan through well and identify the bugs in any situation. When you are conscious, calm, and mindful, you will be able to pick up little hints from the people you mix with. When you sense anyone overstepping or trying to walk over you at work or even in your bedroom, pull up your guards, alert your hypothalamus, and draw a line immediately. Love and compassion are great gifts to give to humankind, but if you are taken advantage of, insulted, or hurt time and again, that zone is toxic, and you better stay away from there.

Finally, be an interesting person yourself to impress others. Everyone wants to be surrounded by people who enrich them with something. Be aware of what you bring to the table and be confident of that. Update yourself with the happenings of the world and your field of work, and have new things to tell people you meet. Driving and interesting conversations can take relationships a long way.

Conclusion

Like a car functions at its best when the engine, the gearbox, the steering, the suspension, the brakes, and all other parts are in sync with each other, a human life can reach its true potential with a healthy body, a strong mind, and an awakened soul. By now, if you have read the book, you will have known that awakening of the soul is not for hermits and ascetics outside the boundary of their domestic world. In this book, we have discussed how your body can be taken care of with little changes in your habits and lifestyle.

The first thing is to know because what you can hold in your mind, you can hold in your hands. When you start believing that you deserve the things you desire, the life force energy of the Universe will come together and create a whirlwind of magic to help you get it all. The first thing to do to reach your destination is to start small. Gather yourself up, sit at a quiet and open place, and then look within yourself. Once you know yourself better and the things you want, you will be in a place to decide the best way to get there.

I would like to tell you a little Buddhist story about the power of the mind, which is the base for the six-pack mind we are talking about in this book. There was a king in a certain kingdom who found it difficult to control his emotions. He would get angry at little things, say things he regretted later, become unpopular among his subjects and court advisors, and end up making wrong decisions for his kingdom. As he grew older and his workload became heavier with an increase in the number of subjects and expansion of his territory, his control went further for a toss. Soon, he realized that his mind was now controlling him and throwing him where it wanted, and he had lost all control of his mind. He decided to step up and work for it. He set off on a journey to explore more of the world, and the first stop was at a neighboring kingdom where the king was known for his wisdom. He stayed the night, and the neighboring king welcomed him with open arms and a grand meal. The king found a fly in his soup and shrieked out in anger immediately. His head became hot, and his face changed colors as he shouted at the workers to get the bowl of soup replaced with a fresh one. The workers got flushed by the reaction, and the ambiance of the party changed into a stressful scenario in no time.

The neighboring king, who was the host, was startled at his reaction. He came and explained to the haughty king that what happened was a minor issue and it was his mind that blew the reaction out of proportion. The haughty king said it was usual for him to get very angry at little situations like that. The host king then explained that situations will not always be in your control, but what you can control is your reaction to that incident. So, instead of shouting and creating a fuss about a tiny fly, he could have thought it through, realized that it was not much of a deal, and calmly asked someone to remove the bowl. The world would have been done the same way, but the collateral damages could have all been avoided.

What is the lesson to learn here? If you feel angry, do you keep your anger suppressed? No. Hold on to your emotions and think hard before you react. Is your emotion justified? If you react how your mind is telling you to, will you do the right thing? Will this reaction make the course of action easier or turn things more sour? If this is not the right reaction, what could be the next best possibility? Think of all these questions and then decide on your reaction. This is a golden rule of life and will help you carve a better way for yourself.

Before we say goodbye, here is a reminder to do to strengthen you in life:

- Meditate at least for 10 minutes every day, to begin with, and push it to a longer tenure as you go. Gather the pieces of your mind together and bring them to one place. Then focus on that spot and try that your mind does not walk around the garden. The more you learn how to focus on one spot during this time, the more you will be able to focus on your goals and also branch out to different innovative thoughts during the rest of the day.

- Talk to yourself regularly and keep yourself updated about your progress and failures in different walks of life. The habit of writing notes of your dreams, goals, progress, failures, reasons for gratitude, and further plans can all give you clarity about your thoughts so you can look back to see how your life is taking shape.

- Exercise physically every day or at least five days every week to keep fit, gain strength in your muscles, and practice your balance. It will help you regulate your weight, fight diseases, look good, inspire others, and plan a growth curve for your old age.

- Practice mental exercises by counting, playing memory games, grounding your mind to the present moment, calming your mind by creating a safe space, and so on. Exercising your mind is as important as exercising your body.

- Practice looking at the mirror and smiling at yourself every day. Wake up and remind yourself of everything you are capable of doing. Live the day like you own it. Place yourself above everything else while being compassionate about others, but not at the cost of your self-esteem.

- Be good to people, and think of every situation from the other's perspective; however, remember to draw and maintain boundaries.

- Eat well, sleep well, and take care of your body and mind. Only you are responsible for your wellness in this world.

So, dear reader, you have the golden rules to live a life as subtle or grand as you like it. The idea is to not define a particular kind of life for anyone. You are unique, and so should be your ways. So, get up, know yourself, and choose the things that are best suited to you. Make the right choices and enjoy the fruits of your labor and faith. Surround yourself with the right people and enrich your mind and life with whatever they have to offer. Cook yourself a meal at home on most days and stuff your body with the right food in the right quantity for good nutrition and a balanced diet. Exercise the right amount, keep fit and healthy, and make sure not to overwork your limbs. Give your body adequate rest, and make sure to stretch and walk in between your working hours, especially if you are sedentary at work. Make new friends and mix with new people with an open mind, but make an effort to keep in touch with people who have always been there.

Be punctual and value other people's time because time is the most precious gift you can give anyone. Be responsible and fulfill the promises you make so that people can grow a certain confidence in you. Grow into the person you have always wanted to have in your life. Not everything is in your hands, but a lot in life is. If you stand at the edge of a mountain and look around, you will see other mountain peaks, valleys, and the vastitude of nature covered in green foliage, rustic terrain, or snow. All of it is given by the Universe to you as a gift. Now, look everywhere and think about how small you are against the tidal forces of nature. Next, shout out your name into crevices of the hills and hear how the word echoes back to your ears. Think about how the Universe returns exactly what you send it, maybe a little diminished, distorted, or in a whole new form. Your being is but a little spot amidst the celestial bodies hanging from nowhere in the Universe. You are not indispensable—no one is. So, whatever you are is for you and some people who care. Remember that and keep them close. Remember that and bring the required changes in your life.

When you wake up, so will your soul. Keep your mind open, your soul awakened, your body active, your health pink, your heart broad, your thoughts and actions conscious, and your life fulfilling. Now that it is time to part, I would end on a happy note. Amidst the organized track of life, make some mistakes and indulge in some chaos. There will be imperfections. Embrace them, smile, and keep walking toward achieving what is perfection for you!

Ready? Seatbelts on. Let us drive through the road of life! The journey might be bumpy, but as long as you choose the right path, the view ahead will make it worthwhile. I promise.

References

Abelsson, A. (2023). *Home Dumbbell Workout (9 Exercises)*. StrengthLog. www.strengthlog.com/home-dumbbell-workout/.

Added Sugar. (2013). The Nutrition Source. www.hsph.harvard.edu/nutritionsource/carbohydrates/added-sugar-in-the-diet/#:~:text=Your%20body%20doesn.

Becca. (2023). *Why Perseverance Is Important: It's Benefits and Development*. Basics by Becca. https://basicsbybecca.com/blog/why-perseverance-is-important#:~:text=Perseverance%20is%20important%20because%20it.

Benefits of Physical Activity. (2022). Centers for Disease Control and Prevention. www.cdc.gov/physicalactivity/basics/pa-health/index.htm#:~:text=Being%20physically%20active%20can%20improve.

Bisht, H. (2022). *Benefits of Tadasana and How to Do It by Dr. Himani Bisht*. PharmEasy Blog. https://pharmeasy.in/blog/health-fitness-benefits-of-tadasana-and-how-to-do-it/#:~:text=The%20Tadasana%20symbolizes%20standing%20strong.

Coronavirus Disease (COVID-19). (2021). World Health Organization. www.who.int/health-topics/coronavirus#tab=tab_1.

Brain Exercises: 13 Ways to Boost Memory, Focus, and Mental Skills. (2019). Healthline. www.healthline.com/health/mental-health/brain-exercises#play-cards.

Chernoff, M. (2013). *4 Short Stories That Will Change the Way You Think.* Marc and Angel Hack Life. www.marcandangel.com/2013/05/21/4-short-stories-change-the-way-you-think/.

Cherry, K. (2022). *How Maslow's Famous Hierarchy of Needs Explains Human Motivation.* Verywell Mind. www.verywellmind.com/what-is-maslows-hierarchy-of-needs-4136760#:~:text=Abraham%20Maslow.

Coronavirus Disease (COVID-19). (2021). World Health Organization. www.who.int/health-topics/coronavirus#tab=tab_1.

Day, D. (2008). *Que Sera Sera* [Video]. YouTube. www.youtube.com/watch?v=xZbKHDPPrrc.

8 Benefits of Balance Training. (n.d.). Primal Play. www.primalplay.com/blog/8-benefits-of-balance-exercises.

Hypothalamus: What It Is, Function, Conditions & Disorders. (2022). Cleveland Clinic. https://my.clevelandclinic.org/health/body/22566-hypothalamus.

Importance of Mental Health. (2020). Vikaspedia Domains. https://www.vikaspedia.in/health/mental-health/importance-of-mental-health.

Innerfully. (n.d.). *Sadhguru - the Story of a Kalpavriksha (Wishing) Tree* [Video]. YouTube. www.youtube.com/watch?v=92_9OYMRzzs.

Jeremy. (n.d.). *Glass of Water.* Emotional Intelligence at Work. www.emotionalintelligenceatwork.com/resources/glass-water/.

Learn about Mental Health. (2023). Centers for Disease Control and Prevention. www.cdc.gov/mentalhealth/learn/index.htm#:~:text=Mental%20health%20includes%20our%20emotional.

Lindberg, S. (2020). *What Are Chakras? Meaning, Location, and How to Unblock Them.* Healthline. www.healthline.com/health/what-are-chakras#the-7-main-chakras.

Longrich, N. R. (2020). *When Did We Become Fully Human? What Fossils and DNA Tell Us about the Evolution of Modern Intelligence.* The Conversation. https://theconversation.com/when-did-we-become-fully-human-what-fossils-and-dna-tell-us-about-the-evolution-of-modern-intelligence-143717#:~:text=Fossils%20and%20DNA%20suggest%20people.

Mayer, J. (2001). Your Body Is a Wonderland [Song]. On *Room for Squares* [Album]. John Alagia

Mayo Clinic Staff. (n.d.). *Balance Exercises: Step-By-Step Guide.* Mayo Clinic. www.mayoclinic.org/healthy-lifestyle/fitness/in-depth/balance-exercises/art-20546836.

Mayo Clinic Staff. (2021). *Strength Training: Get Stronger, Leaner, Healthier*. Mayo Clinic. www.mayoclinic.org/healthy-lifestyle/fitness/in-depth/strength-training/art-20046670.

Medline Plus. (2017). *Benefits of Exercise*. National Library of Medicine. https://medlineplus.gov/benefitsofexercise.html.

Mental Health. (2023). World Health Organization. www.who.int/health-topics/mental-health#tab=tab_1.

9 Benefits of Performing Cardio Exercises Daily. (n.d.). NDTV. www.ndtv.com/health/9-benefits-of-performing-cardio-exercises-daily-4015957.

paramhans. *Maslow's Hierarchy of Needs Theory*. n.d.). BYJUS. https://byjus.com/commerce/maslows-hierarchy-of-needs-theory/#:~:text=Maslow.

Physical Activity - How to Get Ac*tive When You Are Busy*. 2021). Better Health. www.betterhealth.vic.gov.au/health/HealthyLiving/Physical-activity-how-to-get-active-when-you-are-busy.

Preservatives: Uses, Benefits, and Risks. (2021). GERDHelp. www.gerdhelp.com/blog/preservatives-uses-benefits-and-risks/.

Robinson, L., Segal, J., & Smith, M. (2018). *The Mental Health Benefits of Exercise*. Help Guide. https://www.helpguide.org/articles/healthyliving/the-mental-health-benefits-of-exercise.htm#:~:text=Regular%20exercise%20can%20have%20a.

Semeco, A. (2021). *The Top 10 Benefits of Regular Exercise.* Healthline. www.healthline.com/nutrition/10-benefits-of-exercise.

Should You Drink Coffee on an Empty Stomach? (2020). Healthline. www.healthline.com/nutrition/coffee-on-empty-stomach.

Should You Really Begin Your Day with a Cup of Tea/Coffee? (n.d.). The Wellness Corner. www.thewellnesscorner.com/blog/should-you-begin-your-day-tea-or-coffee#:~:text=While%20a%20cup%20of%20tea.

10 Breathing Exercises to Try: For Stress, Training & Lung Capacity. (2019). Healthline. www.healthline.com/health/breathing-exercise#alternate-nostril-breathing.

The 20 Best Cardio Exercises to Do at Home. (2021). Medical News Today. www.medicalnewstoday.com/articles/cardio-exercises-at-home#intermediate-exercises.

The Importance of Patience in Life: 8 Benefits (n.d.). Better Up. www.betterup.com/blog/importance-of-patience-in-life#:~:text=Patient%20people%20may%20also%20experience.

The Relationship between Socialization & Physical Activity. (2019). Study. https://www.study.com/academy/lesson/the-relationship-between-socialization-physical-activity.html.

Tiger. (1970). Yoga Basics., www.yogabasics.com/asana/tiger/.

Trauma Symptoms, Causes and Effects. (n.d.). PsychGuides. www.psychguides.com/trauma/#:~:text=Some%20 common%20emotional%20symptoms%20of.

Torres Burtka, A. (2021). *10 Exercises to Improve Your Balance, Prevent Falls, and Stave off Injury.* Business Insider. www.insider.com/guides/health/fitness/balance-exercises.

Why Self-Love Is Important. (2022). My Online Therapy. https://www.myonlinetherapy.com/why-self-love-is-important/.

University of Glasgow. (2020). *A Brief History of Medicine.* FutureLearn. www.futurelearn.com/info/courses/study-medicine/0/steps/147884#:~:text=We%20do%20k now%20that%20from.

Vivekananda, S. (n.d.). *Swami Vivekananda quotes.* Goodreads. www.goodreads.com/quotes/6493327-the-human-mind-is-like-that-monkey-incessantly-active-by.

What Is Trauma? Effects, Causes, Types, and How to Heal. (2022). Psych Central. https://www.psychcentral.com/health/what-is-trauma#how-to-heal.

Wisdom Insights. (n.d.). *Power of Not Reacting - How to Control Your Emotions | Gautam Buddha Motivational Story*

[Video]. YouTube. www.youtube.com/watch?v=XTqZEb-0tU0.

Witmer, S A. (2023). *What Is Overthinking, and How Do I Stop Overthinking Everything?* GoodRx. www.goodrx.com/health-topic/mental-health/how-can-i-stop-overthinking-everything.

Printed in France by Amazon
Brétigny-sur-Orge, FR